The

Contemplation

Of

Harold

For The New World Emergent

by

Avo Trevino

DORRANCE
PUBLISHING CO
EST. 1920
PITTSBURGH, PENNSYLVANIA 15238

Dorrance Publishing Co
585 Alpha Drive
Suite 103
Pittsburgh, PA 15238
Visit our website at www.dorrancebookstore.com

ISBN: 978-1-6376-4186-6
eISBN: 978-1-6376-4820-9

Cover Art by Troy Lee Sutton
Contributing artists: Troy Lee Sutton & Jule Kurzawa
Contributing poet, Tracy Gwynn

CONTENTS

FATHER'S INSPIRATION

"It will be worthy of a free, an enlightened, and at no distant period a great, nation to give to mankind the magnanimous and too novel example of a people always guided by an exalted justice and benevolence. Who can doubt that, in the course of time and things, the fruits of such a plan would richly repay any temporary advantages which might be lost by a steady adherence to it? Can it be that Providence has not connected the permanent felicity of a nation with its virtue?"

*Excerpt from the 1796 Farewell Address of George Washington, the Commander in Chief of the Continental Army and the first President of the United States.

FOREWORD

Whether 'tis nobler to suffer the slings and arrows of outrageous fortune having dared mighty things to win glorious triumphs, or take rank with those mild spirits who in renouncing the corporeal world have never* realized great marshal victory or defeat, only the good Lord knows for sure.

But whether one finds they are inclined toward action or ideals, it would seem the better part of mankind's remarkable achievements have been ushered in on the sturdy backs of those progressive souls who would not, or could not, accept the status quo.

And so, in the interest of perpetuating the conversation about and attention to the weighty issues troubling the minds and disturbing the peace of our brothers en masse, the following discussion is offered. And of course, these musing are not meant to be an end-all summation, but rather a launch pad and would-be stimulus for further deliberation.

Here's hoping our collective intent propels us all toward the manifestation of our higher ideals, and praying that the world's courageous torch-bearers, wherever they may be, are blessed with renewed strength and the will to ever endure.

Avo Trevino

*(Seldom: Gandhi and (?) ...

DEDICATION

As the Industrial Age gives way to the New Millennium, the pensive spirit of Harold beseechingly petitions for a heightened consciousness from all. Recorded in rhyme, Harold contemplates the sundry concerns of 21st Century man with hope that our collective ingenuity is equal to the maze.

Harold, a Jamaican born grandfather of deep conviction and strong moral fiber was raised with a keen sense of ethical conduct. His opportunity to live abroad in Jamaica, New York, Paris, and Los Angeles helped form his commendable humanitarian perspective. He has served as a valuable inspiration for this offering and is due respect and appreciation.

May his essence of reasonableness, synchronicity, and universality live forever.

PREAMBLE

Sister Moon, stir my Soul

Confucius: **"Would you also revile the butterfly
because you found the larvae objectionable?"**

Now is a time for increased tolerance of things once considered unacceptable. This eminent phenomenon is manifesting in the form of multicultural assimilation and transformation. The former barriers are dissipating into fields of interaction. This condition provides accelerated opportunities to promote universal harmony and understanding. With the increased ability to share mutually beneficial concepts our collective congruity will appropriately emerge.

Emissaries of renaissance unite.

RAMBLIN' MAN

Ramblin' man with pen in hand.
    Bourgeois rap with lessons in sap.
All's been said, and better at that.
    But the words all rhyme, even if they're "braap".

Ramblin' Man: There are many who would say there is nothing new under the sun. And perhaps there isn't. The concerns of modern man would not seem all that different from those of antiquity. To burp them up again may be futile, but then again, maybe not …

1) Is there really anything "new" under the Sun ?
2) Is all the knowledge of the Universe already manifest, and merely awaiting our discovery, or re-discovery?
3) Is "new" knowledge required to solve our existing dilemmas?

I AM

No, I Am
      Yes, I Am not
The answer has me jammed
      So the question I forgot
Its jumbled time on a broken clock
      Its mumbled rhyme with no tick-tock
It listening closely, but hearing no more?

I Am: I AM; God, The Creator, The One Who Always Is, The One Who Always Was. And man, His creation, His protégé; made in His image.

The intrinsic nature of man's relationship with his Creator, and mankind's fundamental mission here on Earth is the source of ongoing speculation, and the cause of considerable consternation. The often perceived disassociation between God and man, and the seemingly perpetual senseless suffering of the world compels significant numbers to abandon their efforts to stay in tune with "Him", while they lead lives of fruitless self-interest.

1) Is God separate from his creation?
2) Is mankind separate from God?
3) Is there an element of God inherent in all men and women?

CALL THE DOCTOR

Ptomaine pain and heaver strain
    Enough to put me off my swill
Another trip to the age of rage
    It seems I've lost my will

Or perhaps my patience is all that's lost
    As I sit so idly by
I hear the rap and all the crap
    While my spirit yearns to fly

Call the Doctor: The world is full of unsavory business, enough to drive one to distraction and despair. And it's easy enough to understand why avoiding the struggle is commonplace. But as a thoughtful man*once said, "All that is necessary for evil to triumph is that good men do nothing". (*Edmund Burke)

1) Does "silence imply consent"?
2) Does mankind have a responsibility to intercede on behalf of his fellowmen?
3) Is mankind ethically and/or morally obligated to be their brother's keeper

VERITIES

It comes to those from whence it's sown
The mystic place of truths intoned
The lessons of Love, despair or woe
Dispensed, unwrenched, from Heaven's throne

Verities: Proceeding from the premise that the Good Lord is the sole source of all that is, including all that constitutes "truth" ...

American poet and essayist Ralph Waldo Emerson, and those of his thinking, believed that a verity, a truth, has an inherent quality, and can be evidentially recognized as such by souls of a discerning nature.

1) In the relative world of Nature, are there verities which would appear to be fundamental?
2) Can "truths" be altered by perception or circumstance?
3) Should the "truth" always be told, or made public?

HANG TOUGH

Since when, since then, time was on his side
Over hill, but crooked still, for the masses he did stride
A man of moral fiber, but lo, of ill repute
His candle burned down to the wick, the works he oft' did shoot
The price was high, but still he found, the score was always tied
For Fate's fair smile is bittersweet, so he hung on for the ride

Hang Tough: The "Fates" as we read, are the three deities in Greek and Roman mythology who are said to determine the fortunes of man through the meting-out of justice, or on occasion caprice, (or at least what appears to be capriciousness in the short run). *In this instance, and pretty much throughout the book, Fate, and the Fates are used to represent Heaven's Justice, based on the even-handed principles of reciprocity.*

1) Is it possible for mortal man, even with his best efforts, to ever become wholly moral while on the earthly plane?
2) If one believes it is "impossible" to become a completely morally correct entity, does this in any way excuse proceeding with the effort to be so?
3) Is a man's fate always just and fair? (His ultimate fate?)

FAITH

A simple turn of locksmith's key?
Ask and it shall be had by thee?
If it's true, pray cautious be
When and what you wish for me

Faith: Jesus is quoted as saying that if your faith was that of a grain of mustard seed you could move a mountain into the sea,* and that if you'll but seek, you will find, and knock, and it will be opened unto you.** The Hindu yogis record beliefs that what your powerful mind truly believes will come to pass, while the creative visualists support that Faith is one of the primary ingredients in the on-going phenomenon or principle of "ideas, desires and dreams made flesh".

1) Is the principle or element of faith a quantifiable commodity?
2) Does science support the proposition on any level, or in any venue or circumstance, that there is intrinsic power in faith or belief?
3) Can ones degree of faith be increased by application or experience?

---

*   Bible; Matthew 17:20 & Mark 12:22-23, (" ... for verily I say unto you, if ye have faith as a grain of mustard seed, ye shall say unto this mountain, remove hence to yonder place, and it shall remove; ...")

**   Bible; Matthew 7:7, (Ask, and it shall be given you; seek, and ye shall find; knock, and it shall be opened unto you.)

AIR CULTURE

Fruitcake etiquette
The world of Air
Verbose dyslexia
Oratory snare

Air Culture: "Hot air", as a symbol of boast, accusation, explanation, or conjecture miss- or over-stated is in some ways congruent with the qualities of the "Air" element in astrological terminology. The gaseous nature of air conforms to any shape, in its static state cannot be seen, felt, heard, smelled or tasted, and, as we all know, is fundamental to our survival.

1) Is "political correctness" essential to maintaining a civil society?
2) At what point, if any, does social etiquette fail to serve the interest of the whole?
3) How does one discern between subtlety or discretion and mere double-talk?

CONSCIENCE

An innocent heart in a starving spirit
Searching vainly for the un-tinted light
Conscience wars with those who hear it
Is it Lord the Master, or demon of night

Conscience: There are those who believe that man begins life as a pure and innocent vessel, a guileless being, only to be corrupted by the temporal nature of the world. And yet it seems man maintains a common element or influence reminiscent of his original sanctity, and that is his conscience; the said innate ability to distinguish "right" from "wrong".

1) Is the phenomenon of conscience a universal principle?
2) Is conscience a personal attribute?
3) Can one's conscience be developed, or lost?

PROCRASTINATION

Can I pay it back over time
      The will to wait is hard to find
Lost again on a road to fun
      Forced astray by the thoughts of some

Time acceleration as day passes day
      More procrastination as spirits decay
In search again for the will to fight
      Backbone jellies as day covers night

Procrastination: Probably as a rule, procrastination is seen as a fairly harmless habit that in general only negatively affects the person guilty of it or those with whom they are closely associated. However, in a broader context, the reality of it impacts us all as the disenfranchised multitudes beseechingly await the intercession of those who might ease their burden in any number of ways.

1) Is procrastination simply a by-product of aversion or indifference?
2) Is it, or can it be morally wrong?
3) Why is it some people seldom procrastinate?

POVERTY

"**Poverty is a state of mind,**
       Shared by all who have a lack"
Semantics only for those well-heeled
       And pain to the bone when its food or a shack

Poverty: Ramshackle huts and starving babies are the all too familiar images conjured-up when one thinks of poverty, and perhaps rightly so. This said, an impoverished spirit may in some ways be as equally disconcerting.

1) Is there a difference between being poor and being "broke"?
2) If one is rich in Love does it, can it, supersede a lack of physical comforts?
3) Does one's awareness of material "wealth" directly affect one's sense of being rich or poor?

LOOK OR LEAP

Expedient yea, efficient nay
>Emotions may judgment sway

Desires burn, passions hot
>Their concerns factors not?

Heed the signs
>Weary and spent

Heart's soft whisper
>Is Love's guidance sent.

Look or Leap: On the opposite end of the spectrum of doing nothing when duty calls, is flying off the handle, jumping to conclusions and rushing to judgment, so to speak. Prodded by the emotion of the mob mentality, history is bereft with a long list of social calamities that might have been avoided had calmer heads prevailed.

1) Does "rash" impassioned behavior equate to immaturity and /or selfishness?
2) How does one differentiate between petulance and the occasional necessity of taking quick decisive action?
3) Given a choice, is it better to fault on the side of action?

COMPASSIONS

Sitting on a mountain thinking
Watching as the ships are sinking
Debating whether to save the crew
And take a chance of drowning too

Compassions: The teachings of Buddha, Krishna, Moses, Jesus, and Mohamed all promote the active empathetic struggle to ease the burden of our fellows in need.

1) What factors spur, or inspire man to move beyond simple pity for the plight of others and onto a determined course of action?
2) Does true compassion contain any element of self-interest?
3) What would be the result if real compassion were a universal sentiment among mankind?

DERAILED

The bell rang out but lo the train
  Steadfast in its track remained
The fires burned and the steam blew hot
  But the conductor cried it was all for naught

For the hills were high
  And the canyons dark
And the engineer
  Wouldn't search his heart

Though his glory lay in a valley green
  Over mountain tops and raging streams
Once he'd tried and once was burned
  Now his fear of pain kept his prize unearned

Derailed: "If at first you don't succeed, try, try again" is a familiar platitude. And though it's often much easier to say than to do, times may be improved if it enjoyed a little more practical application.

1) What force or spirit compels one man to persevere while another gives up the struggle after meeting initial resistance?
2) Does everyone have an innate, albeit in some cases latent, will to endure?
3) What compels man beyond a basic self-preservation mode to a self-improvement mode?

NO PRESSURE

Fourth and one for the ring.
A six-foot birdie putt for the cup.
No time on the clock shooting a one-plus-one
down by a point on the home court.
The seven-ten spare, plus one, for the blonde.
No pressure
So what the heck, place your bet.
It's ten to one on *Run in the Sun.*
No pressure
A thief by decree
A fool by degree
Things for love
A turtle dove
Prices too high
Pies in the sky
Eternal bliss?
Or the devil's kiss?
No pressure

No Pressure: Life is full of various tests and pressures to perform, be they from active participation in the everyday tasks and adventures to the perpetual intellectual discernment as to what is of God, and what is not.

1) Is there too much emphasis placed on being "right", on "winning", and on conforming with societal norms?
2) Are all cultures more or less concerned with group conformity?
3) What role does religion and/or politics play in demanding success and compliance of its members?

AMENDMENT

It's said that a house
Will nary but fall
If the Lord and His sculptors
Aren't building the walls

A foundation seated
On swamp or on sand
Will crumble and tumble
In spite of the plans

Oh well, oh hell,
Of mice and mighty men
The road of well-intentioned souls
Doesn't always round the bend

Blinded by an age of slime
Forfeit yours and forfeit mine
Suffered time for "guiltless" crime
A plea for mercy to The One Divine

Amendment: There are those who promote making and following through on goals and plans, but caution against falling in love with them. It would seem the Universe has It's own agenda, and if ones plan is not in harmony with it, success in that specific regard will remain unattained.

1) Though it may appear so on the surface, is "failure" always a bad thing?
2) Why would God allow mankind to "fail" on such a grand scale?
3) In a world of polar opposites, could success be appreciated without the advent of failure

ONWARD

And so and so
      It's off they go
Muddy waters seen
      To follow the sun
In search for fun
      And crystal water dreams

Onward: You try something. It doesn't work. You try something else. They say doing the same over and over again expecting a different result is one definition of insanity. Moving ever onward would appear to be the mission at large.

1) Why is it some people more than others have a difficult time trying new things?
2) What force or power is it that compels man to "stay the course" even when it has proved many times over to be a futile effort or an unsuccessful method?
3) How does one determine when it time to take alternative action?

LIVE

Bitch, moan, witch's gnome
Cauldron boil, and mad dog foam
Another life conjured from cursed loam
Another spirit on earth to roam
Yea carve your way through sand and stone
And suffer well your long way home.

Live: "To be, or not to be, that is the question ..." It would seem a fundamental principle of world cultures to discourage and/or condemn a self-instituted departure from the earthly plane. Rather, we are encouraged not only to live our lives, (albethey labored with difficulty and despair), but live them well.

1) Is life on earth inherently "cursed" with troubles?
2) Is mankind borne to travail with stoic resolve?
3) Can one know "pleasure" without knowing "pain"?

DUTY

And then to Eve the serpent spoke,
    Why be thee under duty's yoke?
Fear do you to dare and feel
    The pleasures found in rebellion's zeal?
You say to me, 'it can only be',
    While I dream a dream of illusory ...

Duty: There are those who believe in a literal interpretation of the Bible story wherein the beguiling devil serpent prompts Eve to eat of the "Tree of Knowledge"*, while others believe it to be metaphoric instruction. Either way it would seem the lesson at hand is a cautionary implorement to avoid the knowing disregard of one's duty and responsibility to uphold the dictates of established Universal law.

1) Are there a set of God-ordained "Universal" laws at work in the world?
2) How can one differentiate between a Universal law and a secular, or man-ascribed law?
3) When does one's duty to adhere to Universal law usurp their obedience to secular law?

* Bible; Genesis 3: 1-24, (... Therefore the Lord God sent him forth from the garden of Eden, to till the ground from whence he was taken. ...)

SACRIFICE

Pray quiet the speak of duty's fee
    The sacrifice for him or she
For chance be had to lose the Love
    The precious gift from God above

An arrow deep would surely be
    A life without your him or she
Sacrifice for Love, you see
    Is better felt, when sadly seen

Sacrifice: To forsake one's personal desire for the wellbeing of those you Love and serve is one of the elemental mores of familial and social governance. And although this "sacrifice" is often viewed by the uninitiated as burdensome, or as an unfortunate restriction, in reality it is wholly in the mutual interest of all.

1) Are different natures or personality types more or less inclined to be selfless?
2) In the modern world, are females more apt to sacrifice their desires than males?
3) At what point does sacrifice become martyrdom?

THE INNOCENT ONES

Sometimes I wonder, in bed whilst I slumber
　　The thinking behind, what causes the minds
Of women and men, to replenish again
　　A world of ills, of terror and chills,
Of mystery without cure with innocent and pure.

Is it life's longing for itself?
　　Another masterpiece off the shelf?
From a source with a plan? Another noble stand?
　　More lessons in faith, for prince or waif?

Whichever you and yours doth find,
　　In circumstance, in heart and mind,
To be in spirit, great or small,
　　Is a challenge to us all.

The Innocent Ones: The reflective souls of mankind have always tussled with the meaning of life on earth, and why it perpetuates itself the way it does. One of the designs of religious philosophies is to provide answers for these would-be mysteries.

1) Is there a Divine plan and directive to "be fruitful and multiply"* life on earth?
2) If so, does man have any choice in this mission?
3) To what end is mankind "programmed (?)" to propagate his species?

* Bible; Genesis 9:1, (And God blessed Noah and his sons, and said unto them, "Be fruitful, and multiply, and replenish the Earth.")

ADAM MICHAEL

Another Adam born without the help of Eve
Another angel form, Lord Michael, loose and free

The season set by fate. The odds of time and chance
The luck of mortal man, as the players pay to dance
The lovers touched and knew, the chances were but few
Eros came and flew, and the memory 'twill be blue

Mapped is now the course. Will valor shine or feign
Does fire not burn hot, do storm clouds not bring rain
Together Love they'll share, together tears will fall
Pray the growth of two, will be the joy of all

Adam Michael: The advent of single-parent families is nothing new, but unfortunately seems to be all too prevalent. This said, who wouldn't argue that generally speaking, "one is better than none". And though more challenging in the classical sense, this situation does not necessarily dictate a diminished life.

1) In western culture, has the negative stigma associated with children conceived out of wedlock lessoned over the past decades?
2) What is the current social climate regarding these issues?
3) Does the Church or State have a moral duty to assist children without a maternal or paternal parental figure?

PRINCEDOM

Mistress fate and Muses too
Goddess earth and Stars of truth
Pray mold my shape, yea, ply with care
To birth a prince of manner fair.

Princedom: Would that each child born in the world had the attention and resources availed to royal prodigy. A remarkable transformation of the planet would surely take place in short order. These things are obviously not to be, left to the influence of our existent human personnel, but perhaps a similar success could be achieved if, in concert, we were to universally evoke the help of our spiritual mentors.

1) Are there spirit guides and guardian angels actively assisting the endeavors of man?
2) Can their influence be solicited at any time?
3) Why do some cultures promote the belief in these ethereal Beings more than others?

BABY BOOM ?

Abortion ?, Extortion ? A simple apportion ?
In line with decree for the Z.P.G. ?

Baby Boom? In an effort to control the negative aspects of over-population some governments have historically instituted compliance directives in support of a Zero Population Growth model. In essence, they made it unlawful to have more than the specified quota of children per family.

1) Does a government or religious body have any moral or ethical right to limit the number of children people choose to bear?
2) Does it make a difference if the resources available to the population in question are severely limited?
3) Are there any methods for controlling population growth that are universally accepted?

ABORTION

Deception of all ?
The keepers game ?
To spawn or to spurn
The question remains

The moral decay ?
The ethics of new ?
To saddle the many ?
To spare but a few ?

The wisdom of man ?
His folly ? his glory ?
Ponder forever,
For two sides has each story

Abortion: One of the perennial weighty issues continually debated with passion is the topic of human abortion. While some believe it to be a simple matter of a woman's right to choose, others see it is a fundamental principle of the right to life, or right of life. Some advocates of the latter position equate abortion with murder, thus relegating it to a class of "criminal" activity.

1) At what point does (a) life begin?
2) Are birth control methods employed to prevent conception morally questionable?
3) With millions of unwanted and uncared for children already in the world, is it morally questionable to add to their numbers?

EUTHANASIA

They said you would die if tarry you did
Right or wrong, be it ego or id
Seems four will be one in sorrow and pain
The foolish or noble in sunshine or rain

To put off a dream or alter a life
For reason or justice, this martyr or wife
What of the present, is mercy not clear
Will honor be served if mothers not here?

Back to the master, an age old concern?
To wait for another, a new life return?

Euthanasia: A story about a married mother of three whose life hung in the balance during the birth of her fourth child combined the issues of abortion and "euthanasia". Although by strict definition, euthanasia is associated with the merciful death of the hopelessly ill or injured, in this rendering "mercy" was afforded to the surviving children and husband by allowing the unborn child to die and the mother to live.

1) Under what, if any, circumstances should euthanasia be permitted in civil society?
2) Why is there a difference between euthanasia for people and euthanasia for animals?
3) How and why do religious cultures differ in their views about euthanasia?

UNITY VIA CONTINUUM

'Tis morning sun, 'tis evening moon
'Tis Janus cool, 'tis heat of June
Ne're the two, or rather said
Shall meet as one
Save with the dead

The gone as we from earth do know
The places naught our souls to go
Lo one is all, both foe and friend
For natures path reveals no end

Unity Via Continuum: Be it Occidental science or Oriental mysticism, both agree that on an sub-atomic level all of the components of the world are made of the same "non-material" essence; that is an intelligence laden particle /energy wave. St. John the Apostle wrote that *God hath made of one blood all nations of men.** This unity of "flesh" is also shared on a spirit level, as each man is endowed with a soul. The different world religions all promote beliefs about what happens to your soul after death, but they largely seem to agree that the soul is immortal and continues on to one venue or another.

1) Is your soul an elemental portion of God, the Cosmic Consciousness?
2) Does the immortality of the soul support a belief in reincarnation?
3) Do Biblical teachings such as, "If you live by the sword, you will die by the sword" promote a Providential system of reincarnation?

* Bible; Acts 17:26, (And (God) hath made of one blood all nations of men for to dwell on all the face of the Earth;").

REBIRTH

A battered soul finds time to pause
To search for truth, the cure, the cause
The pain of old, the wounds to heal
The heart to mend, rebirth to feel
To leave behind a faceless moon
To sing again a youthful tune
Lo anxious doubt does surely stall
Old hearts yield to new loves call

Rebirth: The concept of being "born again" is familiar to both eastern and western cultures. Whether one believes in an actual physical rebirth, or a spiritual rebirth (as in a "born-again Christian"), there is an attendant period of reflection and/or revitalization before the "new" embodiment is made manifest. This re-capturing of lost innocence and/or Love is also common to romantic scenarios.

1) Why would a soul have to, or choose to be reborn on earth?
2) Are there levels of soul evolvement?
3) In affairs of the heart, why are some folks more inclined to let go of the past and move forward than others?

LONG SUFFERING

And though they wait with restless heart,
For sun to shine and clouds to part
For light to shine and blind to see,
The lost to find, the caged to free
For weak and faint to one day feel,
The peace and strength of Holy Will,
For passions call again to urge,
A flight to "right", our fears to purge
For deadly arrows from Hades bow,
To fall amiss, for naught to go
Illusions wane, and dark stars fall,
And a brighter sun for one and all,

Change will come, though long may take,
Like wistful ripples on a dreamers lake
For the tide is set by the One Who Knows,
The time and place for seeds to sow
The path of each, the road to high,
The destiny of you and I
So comfort take, and solace find,
For truth lives on in heart and mind
And tears someday won't mist our eyes,
For all our spirits will one day rise.

Long Suffering: The world may be changing, but the pace leaves the tender-hearted wanting. And though it is easy to see there is a long way to go, that the ravages of ignorance and tyranny still make their home here, Love and Compassion are eternal. Just as sufficient light always over-comes darkness, so too will Love and Compassion prevail in the end.

1) What purpose could God have for all the suffering in the world?
2) Are one's trials in life always proportional to one's impiety, one's ir-reverence for God?
3) Does suffering necessarily end with your physical death?

DESPAIR

Too deep, too long
Too far gone
Another hero
Up to zero

I slip and slide
Into the tide
My ocean of
Unrequited love

Despair: There are those Transcendentalists who believe that in this world there is only Love, and the deprivation of Love. To remedy any negative situation, all one has to do is infuse the commensurate quantity of Love into the equation. Men, communities, and societies lose hope and become despondent when their need for Love remains unfulfilled.

1) Is it ever really "too late" for a man to change his self-absorbed actions and return to the selfless ways of Love?
2) Is there a viable "substitute" for unrealized romantic Love?
3) Is the Love one receives equivalent to the Love one gives?

TEMPORARY REFUGE

It's a dusty path to lover's lane
With battles fought and dragons slain
I'm cornered now, in hopes refrain
Boxed in tight 'gainst Cupid's reign

Temporary Refuge: As the hims and hers of the modern world go forward searching for their would-be "soul mates" or "soul twins", their ideal is all too often unfound. And so making do as people will, they carry on, often maintaining a spark of hope, (be it ever so small), that their dream partner will someday manifest. Making matters trickier, it is not uncommon for one to believe they have indeed found their true mate, while their present partner does not.

1) Do people actually have "soul mates" or soul twins"?
2) Does each person have only one true soul mate or soul twin?
3) If one is in a "committed relationship" is it wrong to abandon it if your soul mate is found?

MANNERS, HAVE SOME

She was coyly snippish,
Sipping from her snifter.
He was coolly snappish,
And doing so he miffed her.

Manners, Have Some: It is said that manners maketh the man, and that a society is only as civilized as the collective outward expression of its social etiquette. Whether on a personal, group, or world level, it would seem to behoove us all to adopt and adhere to a code of conduct favoring respect and decorum.

1) Should formal principals of etiquette be taught in public schools?
2) As the world becomes more of a collective community, should we become familiar with a variety of cultures?
3) When is "style", if ever, more important than content?

DERISION

Derision, derision
A knock-out decision
The power of thought
To laden and fraught

Break will a bone
From a stick or a stone
But with words do they plunder
And lay me asunder

Derision: The ancient Toltec masters believed the spoken word was a force; the most powerful tool we have as humans, a tool of magic. But like magic, white or dark, it can be used to create or to destroy. Jesus said it was not what went into a man's mouth that defied him, but what came out*. Accepting the principle of "words made flesh", many have faith that a better world can be "spoken" into reality with the proper use of language, by an express verbal acuity.

1) Can words actually be used to hurt, or heal?
2) Is everyone susceptible (some people more than others?) to the influence of the spoken word?
3) Has Western society become overly critical, and seemingly infatuated with verbalizing the petty, sordid, and prurient side of life?

* <u>Bible</u>; Mark 7: 18-20, (" … whatsoever thing from without entereth into the man, it cannot defile him; … that which cometh out of the man, that defileth the man.")

JEALOUSY

On a bad day
In a bad play
The actress in found
Lain prone on the ground
Her malady be
Jealous arrows you see
Deep in her heart
From her lover in part
Shot with a will
For respect to instill
In the heart of the maid
For her passions mislaid.

Jealousy: To say regrettable things or to commit violent acts while under the sway of a jealous rage are so common to human nature that the latter is used and accepted on occasion as a justifiable defense, particularly when the perpetrator is a victim of spousal infidelity. And unfortunately, jealousy spills over into many other areas of life as well. People often feel jealous toward their rivals, or envious of those they perceive as having a material or other advantage over them.

1) Should the temporary insanity associated with a jealous rage be an acceptable defense for criminal behavior?
2) Why would (is) the emotion of jealousy an acceptable excuse while other emotions are not?
3) Is jealousy strictly a "self-centered" emotion?

AD SOLUTION

Another jolly mess
My friends
To test the inner strength
And then
To see what spirit soars to find
The lofty light of Odin's mind

Ad Solution: Though perhaps a bit obscure, Odin (the supreme God and Creator in Norse mythology) is meant to be representational of the Most High God in all of our modern world cultures; Allah, Brahma, Jehovah, Yahweh, and whatever benevolent Cosmic Intelligence one might call on for direction and inspiration in times of need.

1) Can, and will "high-minded" thinking, and an appeal to God's intercession provide the solutions needed to today's global problems?
2) Can mankind successfully function without assistance from God?
3) Is mankind "instinctively" compelled to seek "union" with, and thereby help from God?

SYNCHRONISITY

It will be
To you and me
The coolest cool
That it can be
Fret not you
The way you see
As it will come
When time it be

Synchronicity: There are those who believe that the Universe operates with the perfect synchronized precision of a well-oiled machine. That there is no need for worry or fear, and that Providence has a plan and timetable for all future events. Others, though they may also believe that fear and worry are counterproductive energies, feel that the course of events are not subject to fatalistic pre-destination, and can be altered, mitigated, and improved by the active expression and manifestation of human initiative.

1) Does God contrive to affect coincidences (perceived or not) that serve to regulate the detailed affairs of His creation?
2) Does one's adherence to the cosmic principles of moral and ethical behavior have synchronic positive results?
3) Can the active expression of virtue on a mass scale cause large scale synchronistic changes in the world?

VALIANT

From out of darkness rides the knight
The hero's fate, sacrificial rite
Allegiance vowed, in quest for light
In valour mailed, he renews the fight.

Valiant: Though the word "valiant" often conjures-up visions of princes and knights of antiquity, there are many courageous "warriors" in modern times who bravely travail each day to bring light to darkness, justice to injustice, and Love to the forlorn. Giving up their personal interest for the greater good, these heroic figures all deserve our respect and emulation.

1) Why are some people braver, and more willing to sacrifice than others?
2) Where does one get the strength, the personal fortitude to be so courageous?
3) Is there a difference between bravery and martyrdom?

OH MAIA

A deadly opponent, both subtle and wise
A forest but trees, the keepers disguise
Anchored by feathers as they scale the wall
Delusions abundant, though Love beckons all

Oh Maia (Maya): In Hindu philosophy; "maya" is believed to be the sense-world of manifold phenomena held to conceal the unity of absolute being. It is the "illusion" of limitations and divisions in the immeasurable and inseparable. In this belief system, man is destined to repeatedly wander in the dualistic world of good & evil until aware at last he sheds his maya delusion and reunites his soul with God.

1) If the "material world" is constructed of a "non-material" substance does that mean it can be manipulated by non-material methods?
2) Are there negative external forces actively endeavoring to keep man on earth, to keep him from realizing his true essential nature?
3) What would become of Earth if all the souls of mankind collectively merged back together with God?

BOW ?

" Bow you say ?,
To the inn-keeper's rule ?"

*" Or death by decree.
Shall ye be a fool ?"*

" But will buying my life
To spare flesh and blood
Hobble my chances
When my soul's to be judged ?"

Bow? Jesus said, "For whosoever will save his life shall lose it; but whosoever shall lose his life for my sake, the same shall save it. For what shall it profit a man, if he shall gain the whole world, and lose his own soul?"* It can be a struggle to maintain ones personal integrity in a society of diminished honor; in a world that all too often "rewards" the abandonment of principles with material success. (Or at least temporarily ...)

1) Is the world "fallen" from an originally innocent state and now inherently corrupt?
2) Are there still those in the world who are forced to acquiesce to governmental immorality and corruption or face ostracism or even death?
3) Is it possible to function in a "normal capacity" in the modern world without accepting some element of institutionalized bedevilment?

* <u>Bible</u>; Matthew 16: 25, ("For whosoever will save his life shall lose it: ...")

PRAY

A wiser man once said to the flock,
The powers of heaven could serve as the rock
Anchor your dreams on stars in the sky
The magic, the mystery, the answers to why

For it's the world of the keeper, darkness and death,
Of lessons in faith and struggles for breath
Choked by the madness of horror and pain,
a rainbow chase in a deluge rain

Blinders are worn by more than a few,
Pompous and fat, asleep in their pew.
What of a world where sister and brother,
Die in the street, first one, then the other?

Pray: There are a lot of down and out people in the world. And maybe it can't be helped but there seems to be a lot of it about. And most of the fighting around the globe seems to be about those who "have it", and those who are going without. Perhaps Heaven has already provided us with the solution to these problems via the messages of Buddha, Krishna, Jesus, Gandhi, Mother Teresa, and the untold number of other Saints who have graced our presence. *Application* of the instruction would seem to be the key.

1) Are the problems of the world just too big to solve?
2) Has the average person simply given up trying to help?
3) Why are some people inclined to join the active struggle while others seem content to "look the other way?"

BOSNIA SOUL

One day I was walking, the latest fad
When I met a Czech who wearing plaid
He told me a tale of his neighbor land
And showed me a picture of his uncle Fran.

Both were a memory he had to share
With someone, or anyone who bothered to care
His story was common for modern man
When reason gives way to desperate plan.

For home and family the old man fought
Lost in a tangle of radical thought
His impassioned creed he could not forget
His sixty years of toil and sweat

And so the lines of rage were drawn
With rocket blast and riddled pawn
To us and the world, a reckless waste
To them an honor?, for God and faith?

Bosnia Soul: Blowing-up your enemies children only heightens his hatred and confirms the suspicion in his heart. Under these oppressive conditions it is unrealistic to believe any impassioned man or society will choose to voluntarily forsake their long-held philosophies in the interest of assimilating into, or peacefully co-existing with another group. If all creeds could agree to give-up the part of their belief systems that allows for the killing of the innocent the world would surely be in a much better place.

1) What factor does Faith and Religion play in today's world conflicts?
2) Were the Gandhian principles of effecting change through non-violent methods successful?
3) Although the Geneva Convention framers attempted to establish "rules of etiquette" for warfare, is the expectation of adherence to those rules realistic?

EMINENT DOMAIN

Of wonder, of thought
The life that we've bought
Or stole to our shame
What is eminent domain?

Eminent Domain: The dictionary defines "eminent domain" as a right of a government to take private property for public use by virtue of the superior dominion of the sovereign power over all lands within its jurisdiction. Disputes arise, and have arisen, when more than one "sovereign entity" claims jurisdiction over the same area. And as common are disparities in the value assessed, and compensation paid by one sovereign to another, or by the sovereign to the current /former land owner for the usurped real estate.

1) Is the right of eminent domain based on a fundamental principle of the sacrifice of one or some for the greater good of all?
2) Are there any viable safeguards against the abuse of this "right"?
3) If research or reflection reveals a past injustice in the enactment of this right should the inequity be rectified?

EVIL

What good evil but to propel one towards good.

Evil: Why the world's Creator and Sustainer allows the existence of evil amidst the preponderance of goodness continues to plague and mystify the better part of mankind. Perhaps it serves as simple aversion therapy, or perhaps as some fluctuating variable in a more complicated moral-evolvement algorithm. Whatever the Cosmic purpose, the acute awareness of evil mathematically operates to drive those exposed to it toward the safety and serenity of Divine Love.

1) Is evil the antithesis of goodness?
2) Are there actual evil forces, and /or evil spiritual entities in the world?
3) If Lucifer was created by God as a good arch-angel who later rebelled and fell from grace, is his /its redemption possible?

CAPITAL JUSTICE

Justice and man are troubled in search
To kill is a sin says preacher and church
"An eye for an eye" went out with the Son
Will you sleep at night if you trigger the gun?

Capital Justice: In a world evidentially founded on principles of reciprocity it appears only reasonable (at least on the surface) that human institutions would adopt the practice of regulating or counter balancing "capital crimes" with "capital justice". Many, or even most would likely support this historical method believing it to be the only realistic means of deterrent. This said, it would not appear representative of the Christian directive to "turn the other cheek"*, nor does it seem to heed the warning that "Whoso sheddeth man's blood, by man shall his blood be shed:".**

1) Is the enactment of capital justice, whether on an individual or group basis, a harsh reaction to a "symptom", as opposed to a treatment of, or cure for the cause of the symptom?
2) Are the non-violent, "harmlessness" teachings of Buddha, his Hindu contemporary Mahavira, and Jesus ideal truths meant to dispel incarnate error?
3) Is mankind collectively moving towards or evolving into a non-violent existence?
4) Is the noble standard of human dignity lost, and further violent retaliations promoted when "vengeful" measures are employed against wrong-doers? (As opposed to resisting evil with virtue, forgiveness and the means to reformation and redemption.)

---

* <u>Bible</u>; Matthew 5:39, (" But I say unto you, that ye resist not evil; but whosoever shall smite you thee on the right cheek, turn to him the left cheek also.")
** <u>Bible</u>; Matthew 26:52, (Then Jesus said unto him, "Put up again thy sword into his place; for all they that take the sword shall perish with the sword.")

QUANTUM

Marvelous magic, the higher unknown
Techno advancement, from alchemy sown

A fission division, a release from the core
One nth of the power, of the mystery explored

Quantum: It is said that any sufficiently progressive technologically advanced society is essentially indistinguishable from one of Magic; (a corollary of Clark's Third Law). This assessment is presumably based in part on the ability, or inability of the lay members to explain the causal workings of their societies manifested phenomena. The *use* of these advanced technologies, i.e., for creation or destruction determines their association with "wizardry" and good magic or "sorcery" and the dark arts.

1) What did Einstein say about his part in developing nuclear weaponry?
2) Is technology or magic inherently good or bad?
3) Is the historic misuse of "magical powers" the reason it is not common in today's world?, or is its existence merely a fabrication ?

CONTEMPLATION

WHO THE, WHAT THE, WHEN THE, WHERE THE, WHY THE

Situation constipation, No changes seen procrastination.
Contemplation aggravation, Multiplying my frustration
Palpitation pulmonation, Cardio resuscitation
Fornication condemnation, Another special dispensation

Elevation escalation, Spiritual hallucination
Exaggeration interpretation, Teasing truth with imagination
Elaboration fascination, An evangelical consummation
Revelation deliberation, Pray, who knows the explanation

Contemplation: Notwithstanding the amazing technological advancements made on a material level in some parts of the world, in many circles our spiritual advancement has apparently made very little progress. In these areas the fleshy morass of the carnal world still finds itself in an ugly, unchanged quagmire. The rectification of this obvious disparity in progress will require a free-flowing out-pouring from those blessed with spiritual wealth to those souls who are in need. This mission must include the formulation of practical measures to achieve the desired end.

1) Has moral rectitude generally become passé in modern culture?
2) Is there any correlation between the recent up-swings in Christian Evangelicalism and Islamic Fundamentalism?
3) Do both movements seek to re-establish a basic foundation of moral propriety.

READ DID HE ...

Read did he,
> Books of lore and fancy form
> Of ideas said to be long dead

> So what of mystic spirits charm
> Wisdoms temple or funny farm?

> Pray tune it in from God above
> The myriad face of Wakan's love

Read Did He ... : There are who those would argue that we, the modern West, have systematically "thrown the baby out with the bath-water" with regard to maintaining any respect or appreciation for certain laudable elements of other antiquitous cultures. To limit the diverse expressions of God's Love, would seem to limit the attributes of God Himself.

1) Has the West maintained any recognition and practice of "Native" cultural beliefs or rituals?
2) Is the Environmentalist movement an expression or extension of primitive cultures reverence for Nature?
3) Does God have a limit to His forms of expression?

WAKAN

Broken arrow, sky chief's flight
Mystic spirits, shaman's rite
Vision quest, from night to light
Pursue "the way" with Wakan's sight

Wakan: The Lakota Indians of North America referred to their Supreme God as Wakan. There are and have been many names associated with and designated for the Creator God of this world. It would seem the list is as long as the different groups of peoples who have inhabited Earth. Their common bonds include their belief in a Creator, and their habit of beseeching their Deity for direction, guidance and comfort.

1) Is man inherently compelled to seek contact with his Creator?
2) What methods have men employed to seek union with or guidance from God?
3) Is one method better than another if the result is the same?

ISLAM

Trance world, spirits call
Voodoo virgin's higher law
Prepare the way with drum and song
The road to Allah both hard and long

Islam: At least one branch of Islam promotes the communion of their female advocates with Allah through the use of drums, song, and repeated affirmations. When one is overcome with the Spirit and faints in the wake of enrapturement, they are considered blessed. This ritualistic phenomenon is not unlike some of the native religious ceremonies and is also akin to the "direct contact with God" goals ascribed by proponents of meditative disciplines.

1) Is it possible to attain direct knowledge of God through the application of physical stimulants or disciplines?
2) Why do some western religions seem to be leery or skeptical of this type of practice or ritual?
3) Is "speaking in tongues" the growing movement among western Evangelicals akin to the purported ecstasy of spiritual possession

GLOBAL POMPEII

The fourth of July never saw a sky
That glowed like the one today
With swirling gas and falling ash
Do you remember old Pompeii?

A time of old when souls were sold
To the reaper with staff and robe
But now the flames were not the same
As the mountain is now the globe

Can it be that the earth and sea
Will no longer serve as home
For an age of man who could not stand
To leave well enough alone?

Where will be the new frontier
Can survivors make a stand
When their hopes and dreams and memories
Are strewn among the sands ?

Did Mr. Orwell have a clue
Or maybe Mr. Verne
Will time forget the follies past
Will humans ever learn ?

We feel the shame and fight the pain
As the earth it burns and dies
We watch the fires swell then fade
From our spaceship in the sky ?

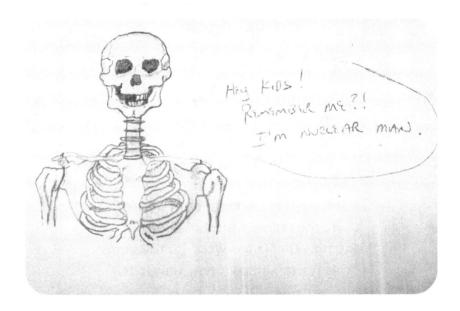

Global Pompeii: There has been a story or two, a movie or three about the devastation of earth and mankind's survival in an all-new venue. There has been talk about colonizing the Moon, or Mars, or space stations orbiting the Earth, Moon or Mars. These dooms-day science fiction stories are perhaps rooted in the darker sagas of earth's history and play on mans fear that reasonableness will one-day lose-out to irrationality.

1) Realistically, in any foreseeable future, are there any new frontiers where mankind could start again?
2) In the matter of mass immorality and its rectification, does the Universe find a way to take care of Itself? (eg, the Bible story of Sodom & Gomorrah)
3) Is mankind "destined" for failure, as suggested by the Bible's Book of Revelation?

CALLING PROMETHEUS

For crimes of mercy, His banishment be
Chained to the middle, Of a boulder at sea
Fallen from grace, Was chosen to be
Caveman's cure, His technology

Diffractory soul, From obscurity freed
Two moments nearer, In the future is he
Our diffident course, Altered will be
Out from under, An eternity

Calling Prometheus: Students of Greek Mythology will remember Prometheus fondly as the Titan who stole fire from Heaven and gave it to the World. This selfless act was done to his own detriment, but, as the story goes, significantly improved the circumstances for mankind. Most would say the world could use a real Promethean figure, someone to enrich us all with another benevolent life-altering parcel of Heavenly favor.

1) Who are the actual heroic souls whose acts or labors substantially improved life on Earth?
2) Will there be any more like them?
3) What kind of scientific or spiritual advances could dramatically enhance our present condition?

GALILEO

Listening to the threat therein
Not knowing if it's wise
To show the others how to begin
To confront all of their lies

Galileo: History has seldom proven kind to those progressive souls who were ahead of their time. Many an advanced patron has endured the dastardly retribution from the lords of established authority as punishment for challenging the status quo. But without that Providential spark, that enlightened inspiration to break through the fetters of conventional thinking and founded practice, the world would see no change.

1) Can one man alone actually change the course of human events, or does it take a collective effort?
2) Is there such a thing as a, or the, "collective conscience" of mankind?
3) What does it take to change the collective conscience of a group, or of the masses?

SOOTHSAYER

Oh brothers of the wandering breed
Windswept vamp of gypsy creed
Crystal, tarot, lines of fate
Future's scroll in nature's state

Visions stolen, or borrowed fair
The curse of truth can sense impair
Fragile forms of mind and wit
Are left preserved in nescient fit

Soothsayer: The old axiom that says "ignorance is bliss" is indeed the case in many instances. This said, the divination arts have been around since time immemorial and are likely here to stay. And although many, if not most people place little stock in fortunes told, a word of caution seems in order for both the practitioners of these crafts, and the would-be seekers of "destined" events.

1) Can anyone actually predict future events with accuracy?
2) Is the future of human events pre-destined to any degree?
3) If the divination arts are so suspect, why have they endured throughout history?

WALKING THE TIGHTROPE

Sometimes I think I see it
And at times, I feel I know it
Ah, but do wish that I could live it

Walking The Tightrope: Walking the fine line between idealism and practicality is a never ending challenge for all the conscientious souls of the world. When the phenomenon is expanded from individual to group levels the differing perceptions as to what constitutes these optimal codes and methods magnifies the complexity of the matter.

1) Why is it seemingly difficult to consistently live by ones guiding principles?
2) Is there only one set of operating principles that represent the pinnacle in thinking and action for all peoples?
3) Does the breadth and magnitude of God's Love demand, or dictate a diversity of expression?

.... IN SEARCH OF THE FINE LINE ....

VIGILANCE

Relentless, tireless, the will to endure
Temptations resisted, the hedonist's lure
It's the life of the warrior, or of ignoble ease
The payday comes later, or now if you please

Beware the illusion, my brothers in sloth
Distinctions are subtle, butterfly or moth
Both from the larvae, but one is of night
One is a treasure, the other a blight

Escape the tethers of the glutton's desire
The ignorant lusts of the agents of fire
Whispers and bullhorns, coos in your ear
From the path of reason do they constantly steer

Vigilance: It seems apparent that on a fundamental level man shares the compulsion of most other life forms; that is the tendency to act so as to preserve their own existence. And even though this self-oriented preservation "instinct" may be of a Natural design, it is often in direct conflict with the restraints imposed by the self-actualized tenets of moral and ethical conduct. Guarding against the surrender to impropriety and excess requires the watchful attention of all.

1) Are the said moral and ethical principles also by design of Nature?
2) Has mankind always been imbued with both instinct and conscience?
3) Is man's conscience actually part of his instinct?

REWARD

For sown seeds and rode miles
Tattered deeds and turned smiles
The limp of age from wanton wiles
Pray your token triggers heaven's stile

Reward: In one sense, the Universe appears to be like a giant mirror, returning to the source the reflections It receives. This operating principle of reciprocity has been observed, memorialized, and promoted throughout time. Be it an adherence to the "Golden Rule": *treat others as you would have them treat you,* an appreciation for the verity, *as you sow, so shall you reap,* or application of the Gandhian platitude that affirms, *the end is inherent in the means,* the conscientious man endeavors to live his life in a style worthy of earning a pass-key to Heaven.

1) Why do some people seem to doubt the premise that one's actions will bring to them their equal measure of just deserts?
2) Are there different "levels" of Heaven, commensurate with one's accumulated good deeds?
3) Does disbelief in an after-life necessarily impact one's actions in a negative way?

TORMENTORS

Tormented from the age of reason
Ghouls and goblins for all seasons
It's Halloween throughout the year
For those of us who harbor fear
To trust in self ability
Will prove to be a choppy sea
Pray put your faith in God above
And harbor not but thoughts of Love

Tormentors: They say on a sub-atomic, metaphysical level the mind is a magnetically charged field of energy. By design, it attracts to itself that which it is broadcasting. As like attracts like, so too does the mind tele-pathically draw to it positive or negative energies. A conscious effort is required to counteract the miasmic forces which compete for dominance and expression. One must actively strive to recognize and expunge neg-ative and destructive thinking in favor of maintaining a mental frame that promotes serenity, peace, and progress.

1) Where do negative and/or evil thoughts come from?
2) Are there actual malevolent entities actively attempting to defile mankind's collective thoughts and actions?
3) Can trust and faith in the power of God overcome all negative in-fluences?

NIGHT TERRORS

Midnight wanes with a waxing moon
With this fear inside my hearts consumed
But alas the curse breaks with the dawn
For with the Sun, the fear is gone

Night Terrors: Anyone who has been intimately associated with the alarmingly inconsolable phenomenon of "night terrors" would surely agree it is indeed a curse. Similar distressing mental and emotional nocturnal trepidations are shared to lesser degrees by far greater numbers. The causal mechanism by which these conditions are alleviated in concert with the rising of the Sun remains to be fully appreciated and explained.

1) What is it about the night that seems to magnify one's fears?
2) Are there correlations between "light and goodness", and the "absence of light and evil"?
3) Is there a relationship between God, goodness, and the Sun?

HELP

Spirits from my past life
Haunt me in the night
Worries for the future
Plague me in the light

Enough of all this trouble
Pray, send an angel bright
To guide me through this journey
And conquer all this fright

Help: According to the teachings of both Hinduism and Buddhism, the force or karmic energy created by the sum total of a man's actions during one lifetime determines the quality and nature of his next existence. Past evils and indiscretions follow one to his subsequent incarnation, where the appropriate measure of torment is administered. It is believed these burdens can be notably diminished by actively renouncing all manner of immoral and unethical behavior, and by making a spiritual effort to live a virtuous life in the here and now. To facilitate these desires, one has only to call upon Heaven's appointed Angels and Guides for assistance.

1) In opposition to the accepted doctrine of reincarnation as expounded by early Christian church fathers (including Clement of Alexandria, Origen, and St. Jerome), why was it declared a heresy by the 6th century delegates at the Second Council of Constantinople?
2) What level or degree of absolution is available to the wayward soul "gone good"?
3) Can one actually, "let go and let God", as they say? (In reference to allowing God and his Advocates to "control" one's life.)

TRAPPED

The horror of man, his fear and his dread
The evil unknown, the place of the dead
Destined by fate, his misery looms
He quakes and he fights, the terror, the tomb
'Tis wicked but known, myopic and pale
The body, the flesh, man's heaven, man's jail.

Trapped: Notwithstanding the assurances of advanced yogis who readily confirm the reality of past lives, future lives, and astral worlds, and the curious seekers who "become aware" of their prior incarnations through hypnosis or past life regression therapies, the average man has no memory of these things and, accordingly, little or no confidence in the veracity of their existence. If he did, he would probably live a more pious life, and be less apt to cling to his present incarnation.

1) If we are all but actors in God's intricate "morality play", why would He magnify the difficulty of delivering an acceptable performance by blocking our recollection of past lives lived and past lessons learned?
2) To what degree would the condition of the world change if mankind as a whole "knew" that their deeds would result in a commensurate "next life" reward or punishment?
3) If an "enlightened" mankind was still imbued with "human nature", is there any guarantee the world would experience a significant change?

CHARON

With pole in hand and face to bow
The river Styx my mate does prowl
Another charge has sensed chagrin
And into the murky waters dove in ...

Of little use will prove the plunge
For his "lifes" been had and his "deaths" begun
The time and chance for barter passed
His penance set, his dies been cast.

We see the wretch a furlong down
And change our mood the malefactor found
We sidle to port, and load him in
I inquire with mirth if he fancied his swim
His anguish apparent behested a sigh
From our reticent host who lowered his eye,

"Perhaps your repentance will alter your stay.
Perhaps your remorse will shorten your days
Perhaps it will only disgust your new lord
Perhaps but a flinch you ill can afford
Be it fickle or fair, it's a call for the Fates
Know well your dilemma as you enter Hell's gates."

So in silence he sat 'til we reached his new berth
Then willfully pliant, accepted his dirge
As we moved away through thickened air
The querulous wails of banshee cheer
I wondered aloud if it possible be
To alter one's time by plea or decree

"Should the Angels of Heaven pity your soul
If Saints and their Sisters would stand in a row
And all pray for acquittal to Pluto and Dis
A reprieve may be granted from the devil's abyss
Though were I another, I wouldn't to chance
Leave my future in question
"Til the torturer's dance."

Charon: In Greek mythology, Charon was the ferryman who transported the souls of the dead across the river Styx to Hades. Though not everyone believes in a physical place designated as "Hell", a quick look around at the modern world reveals that *it* encompasses a wide array of experiences. This diverse range includes those that are diametrically opposed to each other and seemingly representational of the heights of Heaven, the depths of Hell, and everything in between.

1) At what point in time of one's life is their future existence or incarnation determined?
2) Is there such a thing as "a point of no return", beyond which all efforts toward redemption are fruitless?
3) If the Universe is regulated by an exacting "Cause and Effect" /"Just Deserts" reward system, wouldn't any and all acts of contrition impact one's future state?

DISTANT FLAME

The call from a distance, The light of the soul
A heart yearning daily, For what angels must know
Scented with romance, The candle of Love
Softly it whispers, The coo of a dove
A vision of pureness, It's flickering glow
Blissfully calming, Though flames take their toll

Distant Flame: It would seem that as a collective unit, mankind does a lot of "pining" for Love; be it familial, romantic, or Divine. The longing for assurance that one is truly cared for by family or paramour appears to be a universal compulsion, and is perhaps derivative of man's greater need for certainty that he is intrinsically connected to, and beloved by his Creator. And yet, at least on this plane, the beneficence of Love typically comes affixed with a "price", exacted from its mortal practitioners in varying degrees and ways.

1) Is Love one of the essential elements on which the world is founded?
2) Could the human species survive at all without the advent of maternal or paternal love?
3) Is one's suffering, as a result of a Love-loss, necessarily proportional to the intensity to which they loved?

MAKE A MOVE

As I sat in the dark
Awaiting a spark
From Providence to show me the way
A notion I had
While feeling some bad
That perhaps it would all change today

"Have courage", said I
As I looked to the sky
To bolster my waning reserve
A move I would make
With my "safety" at stake
Though victory is not without nerve

Make A Move: It is said that each of us here on Earth has a purpose, a mission, a calling if you will. Part of the individual's quest is to recognize this unique function and work toward bringing it to fruition. The difficulty faced by many lays in understanding and accepting what their given task is, and further, if and when it is perceived, taking proactive steps to break free from their securely rutted path of lesser meaning to manifest their higher divine destiny.

1) How does one go about identifying what their mission is?
2) Does everyone have the same or similar calling?
3) Are we all, eventually, meant to be "gods", and, as Jesus said, to do works equal and greater than what He did? *

* Bible; John 14:12, ("Verily, verily, I say unto you, He that believeth on me, the works that I do shall he do also; and greater *works* than these shall he do; because I go unto my Father.

CARPE DIEM

Here I sit, bent and curled
Viewing life as it unfurls
Sitting fetal by the hearth
As licking flames leap up from earth

The fires life, from staid repose
To fruitions form, then out it goes
Much the same the mortal spirit
So seize the day without fear of it

Carpe Diem: This Latin term, translated as "seize the day" or "pluck the day" is in one way an inducement to enjoy the pleasures of the moment without concern for tomorrow. Although the imbalance of this is seen as imprudent or wanton, the positive element of this sentiment is held to be an encouragement to make the most of your given situation. To go forward with confidence and faith that God will inspire, nurture and support His devotees throughout the course of their limited life on Earth.

1) Does Jesus' instruction to worry not about the concerns of the day, seek first the kingdom of God and all material things will be provided for you parallel the positive aspects of the carpe diem philosophy? *
2) Can confidence that one will endeavor to serve God and His Universe dissolve any fear or anxiety about moving from a dormant posture to a state of action?
3) How does one balance the "need" to "save for a rainy day", while at the same time live for, or in the moment?

* Bible; Matthew 6:25-34, ("Therefore I say unto you, take no thought for your life, what you shall eat, or what ye shall drink, … Take therefore no thought for the morrow; for the morrow shall take thought for the things of itself. …)

CINDERELLA MIDNIGHT

Let's do something, even if it's "wrong"
This waiting games gone on too long
Say, make your move
Pray, try your luck
But do it now
Before the clock has struck

Cinderella Midnight: Hindsight often reveals an array of missed opportunities. And although there is a time for all seasons, a time to be still, and a time to take action, perhaps a more action-oriented approach would serve to increase the potential of realizing the positive manifestations of personal and societal needs and goals.

1) Does a "body in motion" always stay its course until acted upon by an outside force?
2) Can one's own initiative be the "outside force" needed to compel a different course and direction?
3) How does one go about birthing, developing and increasing their enterprising force, inventive energy and ambitious drive?

ACTION

Look and leap
Wait and lose
Fate is fickle
To ye that snooze

Action: A man can't afford to laze about while there's work to be done lest he wind up like the destitute grasshopper in Aesop's fable. Neither can he execute a successful operation without the proper preparation. Both examples promote appropriate action: ie, those endeavors associated with formulating a plan, and those integral to carrying it out.

1) Do some opportunities to take action only come around once in a lifetime?
2) How does one avoid the phenomenon of "analysis paralysis"?
3) Does every action have an equal and opposite reaction

ERRORS

Remember well but suffer not, past errors in your game
As the gone-by lives of all mankind, are dark with many shames

Errors: They say, "to error is human, to forgive is Divine". The trick to moving forward often lays in forgiving yourself (not to mention others) for past miscues. There are many examples of individuals and groups who made their share of "mistakes" before becoming successful. "Learning" from failure is of course recommended, while dwelling on past errors should be strictly limited.

1) Why do people, (society in general?) seem to focus on pointing out the mistakes of others?
2) Does this preoccupation serve any useful purpose?
3) Why is it an error committed can ruin one person's "whole game" while another can "shake it off" and move on to continued success?

REALISM

Shoot for the stars
Take Venus or Mars

Realism: The line of reasonableness between idealism and realism is fluid in nature, ebbing and flowing with the dictates of time and circumstance. It is said that progress is made by exploring and pushing the boundaries of established norms. However, in this effort, the governing principles of prudence and order should assure the maintenance of practical necessity.

1) Can a world culture, striving to evolve into a more civilized expression, harmoniously function without being founded in pragmatism?
2) What are the sources of inspiration that propel man from the utilitarian to the visionary?
3) In the interest of accelerating this transformation to a higher state, how can we magnify and optimize the divine element of visionary inspiration?

ONCE MORE

> Lovers and life
> Hatred and strife
> One Time Only
> Is the flip side of Twice

Once More: For those who have suffered from "Love-loss", be it through death, divorce, or some other circumstance, it often feels like a permanent condition wherein relief from the grief appears distant at best. These feelings are completely understandable, and commonly shared. However, Nature is not without heart, and for those who can manage to keep theirs open, new Love can be found.

1) Is an aversion to "Loving again", be it temporary or permanent, in part a self-preservation instinct?
2) Are there any established parameters for "periods of mourning"; before one allows them-self to become involved in another Love relationship?
3) Are there any circumstances where it would be considered inappropriate to Love again.

THANKS

And from the blue an amber hue
    The blissful calm of moods anew
Respite found in battles lull
    A breath of life for heart and soul
Pray give thanks for comforts found
    The soothing touch of Love's renown

Thanks: In times of on-going conflict (even in war) there are moments of compassion. These interludes into civility, empathy and concern are representative of the healing rays of Divine Love. And though these respites are all too brief in many cases, they serve to confirm that the reality of Love's ideals forever endure. Would that we could stay ever-focused on them.

1) By what spirit are men amidst wars prompted to call for a "cease fire" on their respective religious Holydays?
2) Was Einstein right when he said?, "Any intelligent fool can make things bigger, more complex and more violent. It takes a touch of genius, and lots of courage, to move in the opposite direction."
3) Do people at times maintain contrived positions or postures of conflict with others as a means of "self-protection", as a simple need or desire for limited interaction with their antagonist?

SO LONG

So long oh ye tired of yore
Fare thee well
And mourn thee no more
Take heart as the new
Burst through from the blue
To balance the proverbial score

So Long: Jesus said, "Blessed are they that mourn, for they shall be comforted."* His apostle Paul followed saying, "And let us not be weary in well doing; for in due season we shall reap, if we faint not."** Those who believe we can, and do, actively create our own circumstances advise that knowingly releasing one's attachment to the negative past accelerates ones manifestation of a positive present and future.

1) Along with doing "good works", do we also have a responsibility to society to "think good and positive thoughts'?
2) Does forgiveness of past transgressions (against an individual or group) play a part in being able to create a new and improved condition?
3) Does "good" happen more to people that expect it?

* Bible; Matthew 5:4, ("Blessed are they that mourn: for they shall be comforted.")
** Bible; Galatians 6:9, (And let us not be weary in well doing: for in due season we will reap, if we faint not.

SIRIUS: THE DOG STAR

In days gone by, the sweep of time, the vision of a love sublime
      Played upon my memory track, now new moon brings the
      angel back
A fire maiden with eyes alight, and passion hot to fill the night
      Innocent charm, the sultry rose, wistfully my longing grows
In times of yore my soul said nay, I couldn't give my heart away
      But now when Eros aims his bow, alas my mentor deems it so.

Sirius: The Dog Star: "Star light, star bright, I wish I may, I wish I might ..." The brightest star in the heavens (night sky) is Sirius, of the constellation Canis Major. In the best of romantic terms, the brightest star in a married man's "heaven" is his wife, his partner, his paramour and confidante.

1) Can one's heart, one's soul, be relied upon to guide them in choosing their spouse?
2) Are "marriage unions" sanctioned in heaven by angels, gods, or spirit guides?
3) Is "timing" always a factor when deciding to enter a contract of marriage?

SHADOWS

To own a soul is nay to right
  This nature's call shadows light
A partner yes, but trinket not
  Remember wounds from battles fought
Proud and strong the sapling tall
  If not rooted where shadows fall

Shadows: Save for perhaps the familial obligations of children, the immorality of involuntary servitude appears obvious. This stated, on a less severe level there are those who seem to gravitate toward controlling the actions of others. The imbalance of this propensity can impede the growth and well-being of the subject(s) laboring under the over-bearing weight of subjugation, domination, or tyranny.

1) Are some natures more inclined than others to want to be the boss, the one in control?
2) Does, or should, one's sex have any bearing on one's capacity to lead?
3) Do some people prefer to be followers, to be directed, or even controlled by others?

I DO ?

They swear by the law
        Through thick and through thin
Building houses of straw
        For partings no sin

Whereof the rules
        By which we stand
Design of heaven
        Or madness of man (?)

I Do?: It is said that nearly 50% of marriages in the United States of America end in divorce. This would seem to reveal a marked casualness and an overt lack of seriousness with respect to honoring the sanctity of the wedding vows and the traditional institution of marriage.

1) Why are so many people in western culture so quick to give up on a marriage and get divorced?
2) Is divorce a by-product of an affluent society?
3) Does the propensity of divorce reveal a general decreased parental concern for the well-being of the children involved?

FATES

Soar do the Faeries
The Muses my friends
Help me oh sisters
From falling again

Fates: The fabled benevolent beings said to grace our days are kept alive in the mythologies of man. In theory these high-minded, God-ordained entities are willing, ready and able to guide the paths of those human seekers of peace, truth and beauty. Akin to the angels, they are our "sisters" all.

1) Is there any factual evidence to support the existence of such mystical ethereal beings?
2) Why does every culture contain folklore about these entities if their reality is not founded in some element of truth?
3) Can a general disbelief in an unseen presence effectively dissolve, suspend or annul its existence?

LA GUARDIANS

They've got a fix on you
    They've got a fix on me
The silent band of lesser gods
    From beyond what we can see

The mystic place of truths
    Legends and decrees
The heavens found for mates renown
    Our mentors, he and she

La Guardians: It is said that everyone, especially children, have guardian angels assigned to protect and watch over them during their time on earth. Working in concert with our conscience, these celestial entities are believed to "walk beside us" and guide us, their numbers surpassing those of the human souls on earth by a substantial sum.

1) Do the Bible, the Torah and the Qur'an all support the existence of a variety of angels, and angel-like beings?
2) Is it possible to make contact with and /or see ones guardian angel(s)?
3) Can one develop their awareness of and relationship with their guardian angels?

A THANKS GIVEN

Once upon a T-day dreary ...
    A grayish wind amongst a flurry
Came tersely ripping at my clothes
    The barge of November's icy throes

I see turned to brown the golden leaf
    Beclaiming Autumnal season's grief
And salute a thanks to harvest's store
    The foil of winter, pray, evermore

A Thanks Given: In the affluent west, it is easy to forget just how good we really have it. With our grocery store shelves consistently stocked, the ravages of Winter seem but a vestige of the distant past. However, even a small amount of world travel makes one more grateful for our abundance, and clearly illustrates the overt disparity between what is, what could be, and hopefully one day, what will be.

1) How is it that America enjoys so much abundance compared to the rest of the world?
2) Does Divine intersession influence this favored state?
3) Does great wealth demand great responsibility to share with those less favored?

CHRISTMAS

Christmas time for one and all
 Be it known or not
Matters but a fraction
 If the highest ideals are sought
Day by day throughout the year
 By the players in the show
For it's said that a man's heart be fated
 By *all* the seeds that he has shown

Christmas: The Christmas season and its attendant "spirit" is a blessed thing, where in many cases wars temporarily cease, Charity revives, and people in general are guided by the better angels of their nature. If men were judged only by their thoughts, words and actions during this season they would likely fair alright. But alas they say this is not the case.

1) Though some folks seem to manage, why is it so difficult for most people to maintain the "Christmas spirit" in day-to-day living throughout the years?
2) Does the annual manifestation of the Christmas Spirit provide evidence that mankind is capable of living on a higher plane of civility and compassion?
3) Are the elevated attributes of the "Christ Consciousness" more accessible during the holidays because of peoples focused attention?

X-MAS

Another mass for Christ
    Another time to pause
Another time to show your heart
    Be it Scrooge or Santa Claus
Another chance to see the world
    In its splendor and its gore
Another chance to feel the shame
    For the excess we implore
Another Sun to hide the Moon
    And hold the night at bay
Another time for earnest prayer
    That help be sent our way

X-mas: There are those who complain, and perhaps rightly so, that Christ and the true spirit of Christmas are often missing from the over-commercialized version we see and participate in. Even the name occasionally ascribed to the celebration, "X-mas", leaves some feeling that Christ has been "x-ed" out of the formula. And though historically this of course is not the case ("X" is the Greek symbol for Christ from their letter "chi', the initial of *Christos* / Christ), it is easy enough to see why there are those who might believe this way.

1) As some would ask, how did a solemn mass for Christ turn into an over-indulgent ode to materialism?
2) Does the modern Christmas celebration resemble the ancient Roman Saturnalia in some ways? (Saturnalia was the ancient Roman festival of Saturn, beginning on December 17th and often marked by unrestrained celebration, excess, and extravagance.)
3) How do you suppose Jesus would wish for his birth to be commemorated?

IMAGINE

Imagination, figmentation
    Paradoxical consternation
Doubtless, hopeless ?
    Forever moatless ?
The poor cry out
    But the rich ignore this

Imagine: It is quite easy, and fairly common, for the saddened, piteous, and well-intentioned to stand on the proverbial "soap-box" and bewail the plight of the down-trodden. Though many believe there will always be the poor of the world, others feel it is merely a temporary condition, subject to alleviation by means of desire and collective will. Maybe so. But if there is a cure-all for destitution, it would appear neither simple nor ready.

1) Has there ever been a time in recorded history when there were no "poor people"?
2) Does one system of government (Capitalism, Socialism, Communism, etc.) minimize the advent of poverty among its constituents more than another?
3) On a world scale, are the percentages of those considered impoverished increasing, or decreasing?

UH, WAITING FOR HELL ?

If it were well, tolls of a bell
If it will sell, written to yell
Gark and Aghast, brothers in smell
And you my friend ? Waiting for Hell ?
Aye ?
We knew that you were.
What ?
You're disappointed in who ?
Sorry mate. We thought it was you.

Uh, Waiting For Hell?: Judging solely by outside appearances, some people are just no dang good. The sum total of their actions would seem to be heading them straight for the Gates of Gahanna. As it says in the Quran (Koran), "He that does right, does it for the good of his own soul, and he that does evil, it shall recoil on him."* And yet, becoming aware of the perception of others *can* at times influence ones outlook and effectively change the course of their ways.

1) Are some people just "born bad" and destined for Hell, or is perspective, and its associated actions, formed from one's life experience?
2) Why do some folks seem to feel that they can perpetrate "evil deeds" with impunity?
3) What prompts one man to respond positively to a "moral wake-up call" while another pays no heed?

Koran: Fussilat 41:46, (He that does right, does it for the good of his own soul, and he that does evil, it shall recoil on him.)

WESTERN TROUBLES

They thought their life was laissez-faire
With money to burn and time to spare
But their needy peers thought them crazy
And considered their politics fairly lazy

Western Troubles: *Laissez-faire* is a French term used to describe a doctrine opposing governmental interference in economic affairs beyond the minimum necessary for the maintenance of peace and property rights, and /or a philosophy or practice characterized by a deliberate abstention from direction or interference, especially with individual freedom of choice and action. Many would argue that much of the malcontented behavior seen around the globe stems from the reality or perception of economic inequality.

1) Do our current Western governments operate according to laissez-faire principles?
2) Do governments have a responsibility to all of their citizens to function beyond the mere minimum levels needed to assure peace and order?
3) In the emerging world community can the governments of wealthy nations afford to ignore the financial deprivation of poorer nations?

COMPLACENT SATIETY

Jukebox junkies, flying high
    Cold war flunkies, biding time
Beware the mask, the face of ease
    Your desires quelled, your senses pleased
Your wealth by stealth oh privileged ones
    For penance served when all is done

Complacent Satiety: Someone once wrote something to the affect of, 'In modern times there's only the struggle, while yet my eyes see far and wide distraction from and aversion to the practical rigors of the task at hand.' It's pretty easy in the West to put in your eight hours, go home, grab a bite, a drink, and a smoke, and then zone-out in front of the TV, essentially shutting out the rest of the world.

1) If a man, in good faith, performs his allotted daily task in diligent fashion, does Providence "require" an additional charitable effort?
2) What standard should be used to measure the requisite contribution to the global cause mandated of the conscientious world citizen?
3) Does an uninformed, naïve, or "innocent" man inherit the "negative karma" of his /a corrupt employer, church, town, or country?

ZEALOUS ABATEMENT

From dusty floor and tattered wall, the cure is found for one is all …

The blessed oppressed take hold the day, the given chance will squander, nay
Up from depth of mendicant way, to face the test of moral malaise
The season ripe for growth to speed, newly found "the merchants creed"
"Industrialize" the modern seed, to forever stave the rural need
But quickly pass do peoples all, from urgents drive to comforts lull
Once attained the treasured hall, a facile prey the hunt does stall

Zealous Abatement: It would seem the physical world and its affairs operate in given phases, periods and ages. It's a new moon, a full moon, and a lunar eclipse. It's your today, their tomorrow, and everybody's yesterday. Headlong we cycle through the varied experiences and myriad lessons, eventually emerging to find the Measureless End.

1) Given the capacity, why does an awareness of unrealized material comforts motivate some people to take action to achieve them and not others?
2) On a societal level, how does the prevailing or emerging group work ethic typically dictate the methods of the majority population?
3) Why does the accumulation of wealth, and/or the advent of attaining wealth through easy measures, seem to fundamentally equate to a break-down (or relaxing) of moral and ethical standards /principles?

EQUILIBRIUM

The balance swings,
Hither and yon
Today it's elation
Tomorrow it's gone

Equilibrium: Maintaining one's balance amidst ever fluctuating influences and ever-changing circumstances can be a challenging proposition. Rolling with the punches is often easier said than done. However, with time, experience, and the accompanying perspective, it would appear the Universe *perpetually levels itself.*

1) Why is it the Universe has a way of throwing "monkey wrenches" into the works just when things seem to be going well?
2) Does every human have a story of loss, disappointment or woe?
3) Does maintaining a sense of "even-mindedness" (as the yogis promote) diminish the "passion" of life?; (by suppressing the jubilation of gain in concert with minimizing the depression of loss.)

BRASS RINGS

They say patience is a virtue
So why the heck am I
Chomping at the bit
Each time the ring swings by

I want to grab it quickly
Before it gets away
Forgetting that tomorrow
It again will swing this way

Brass Rings: "Rich opportunities", or "the opportunities to be rich" usually enticingly dangle just out of reach of the average man. Or do they? Some believe the world is forever chock-full of God-provided, God-inspired, and God-ordained vehicles to manifest wealth and luxury. It is but mankind's business to collectively recognize and materialize these offerings.

1) Is "luxury" man's natural state?
2) When Jesus said it was the "Father's good pleasure to give (his devotees) the Kingdom" was he also referring to the material riches of the physical world?* (In association with spiritual riches)
3) Is it anything other than the "power of God" that sustains mankind?

* <u>Bible</u>, Luke 12:32, (Fear not, little flock, for it is your Father's good pleasure to give you the kingdom.)

MAMMON

Problems aplenty
Ill gotten gain
Searching for treasure
All ends up the same

Mammon: "Mammon", a Biblical word of Aramaic origin, is defined as "possessions, riches or material wealth, especially as having a debasing influence." Jesus said a man could not serve two masters equally. "You cannot serve God and mammon."*

1) Is, or can, material wealth be "bad" in and of itself?
2) What does it mean to *serve* mammon?
3) Can a man ever be truly "rich" without being rich in God's spirit? (God's spirit meaning individually or collectively; the Holy Spirit, Loves' Spirit, Christ's Spirit, Christ's Consciousness, Buddha Consciousness, Krishna Consciousness, the Spirit of Allah, or the Spirit of Enlightenment.)

---

* <u>Bible</u>, Matthew 6:24, (No man can serve two masters; for either he will hate the one, and love the other; or else he will hold to one, and despise the other. Ye cannot serve God and mammon.)

"THERES GOLD IN THEM THAR HILLS"

Stories are told, Visions of gold
Hidden and old, Sought out and sold
Another day, Brings more to play
Many, they say, with lives will pay

Jumping the claim, Weak turns on lame
Conquest brings fame, all guile, no shame
A moral decline, booty and wine
Ethics for swine, as yours becomes mine

"There's Gold in Them Thar Hills": Balzac, the 19th Century French novelist and playwright was quoted as saying, "Behind every great fortune is a great crime." And though this sentiment may unfairly besmirch the reputation of the truly enterprising, honest, and diligent, history is bereft with a litany of "claim-jumpin' scalawags who murdered and stole their way to fame and fortune. And some would say it's easy to understand why. For people as a whole have a fairly short memory, and the guilty scoundrels and/or their heirs are too soon revered and envied for their wealth and the social status it affords, while their past crimes are quietly forgotten.

1) Does the possession of wealth, on either a personal or societal level, require a certain portion of charitable beneficence on the part of the owner in order to garner their peers Love and admiration?
2) In the minds of most people, does beneficence on the part of the "criminal rich" absolve them of their original sins to attain wealth?
3) What does it say about a societies collective morality when wealth is valued more than righteousness?

TIT FOR TAT

Tit for tat, This and that, Monkey dung and spit
The days a drag, The hours lag, I wish we all could split

Mush, mush, Dogs and sleds, Rubber biscuit stew
The gold is there, The questions where, Waiting just for you

Power, power, On the hour, The minutes tick away
See the "faint of heart", At the shoppers mart, While the ruthless steal
the day

Tit For Tat: They say in the end, "life is short", but it doesn't feel that way
when you're trapped in a cycle of primal revenge, aimless boredom, or ab-
ject poverty. And though the Universe is a veritable cauldron of power, its
development and appropriate application to worldly affairs could use a
major boost.

1) Is economic disparity a driving force in the mal-contentious actions
   of many militant groups?
2) Is money (and the callous quest for it) really the root of all evil?
3) Is there is a misappropriation of available resources, or a deficient
   effort in manifesting and disseminating those resources that are
   available?

RENUNCIANT

When I was young I thought the world
    Revolved around me alone
In selfish strut I preened about
    Comfy on my throne

But as I grew I came to find
    My world was slightly less divine
For all around my gilded cage
    I saw the face of want and rage

So now, resigned, I struggle on
    Knowing that when I am gone
I lived my life by a friar's tome
    For all the souls who call earth home

Renunciant: To renounce the carnal interests of the flesh and physical comforts of the material world in the interest of dedicating one's life to the pursuit of God and His works is a tradition adhered to and followed by holy men from all ages and all parts of the world. An abdication or abnegation of one's personal wealth may help materially and spiritually bond the renunciant with the downtrodden masses but would appear impractical for the every-day man.

1) Though showing practical sympathy toward those in need may help dispel the darkness of separation between souls, one must ask, "how much is enough"?
2) Is a man any under compulsory spiritual obligation to give away all or most of his personal wealth?
3) Does a man need a pulpit to serve God, or can he serve Him with what he has from wherever he is?

SEE THE LIGHT, DO WHAT'S RIGHT

Skippy and Dickey sat on the stoop
Drinking their English and talking their poop
Skippy was scheming to get him some dope
While Dickey was dreaming of a Nancy to grope

When from out of nowhere they both saw a light
Then quick as they saw it, it slipped out of sight
Dickey returned to his vision divine
But Skippy decided that now was the time ...

See the light, do what's right

See the Light, Do What's Right: Life-changing events come in a variety of packages, from spiritual epiphanies to near-death experiences. One would hope that sometime during their life they will be called by the powers of Heaven to adopt and live thereafter by the principles of practical moral rectitude.

1) Why is it two people can experience the same dramatic occurrence but only one will be moved to significantly change their life?
2) When the Bible says, "there is a time for every purpose under heaven" does that mean that the time-table for a man's "(re)turn toward God" is predetermined to some degree?*
3) What force in nature causes a man to continue to operate in a fashion detrimental to his being even after he has been exposed to higher principles?

---

* Bible, Ecclesiastes 3:1, (To everything there is a season, and a time to every purpose under the heaven;

PATIENCE

I never liked to wait in line
    It always seemed a waste of time
This is not the pace I need
    A man like me is built for speed

But I guess I'll have to settle down
    Clip my wings, befriend the ground
Pick my spots to soar and glide
    And from my duty pray not to hide

Patience: On a personal level, it would seem no one likes to wait much, whether it's for your "big break" at work, the arrival of your "true love", or in the grocery store checkout line. And on a broader plane, to manifest forbearance in the face of provocation and strain, and steadfastness despite opposition, frustration, and adversity is no simple matter either. The desire for instant gratification, along with the expectation of instant understanding and /or assimilation from others is often overwhelming. But as Jesus said, it is through the application of patience that the good fruit is brought forth.*

1) Can our collective impatience be lessened (via a more expedient manifestation of what we desire) by simply focusing more attention on our given goals?

2) Is it true, as postulated by physicists, that on a *sub-atomic level*, an energy wave becomes a material particle only through the advert of observation, by focusing attention on it? (Before observation /attention is focused on them, material particles are said to be mere *energy waves /unobservable probability amplitudes* in the field of infinite possibilities.)

3) Can one's capacity for patience & understanding be increased by simply asking God for more?

---

* <u>Bible</u>, Luke 8:15, (But that on the good ground are they, which in an honest and good heart, having heard the word, keep *it*, and bring forth fruit with patience.)

POET'S PERPLEXTION

I can't seem to figure it out
What's a man to think about
Should I dwell on thoughts of Love
Of noble lore from up above
Or must I spend my waking time
On earthy matters less sublime

Poet's Perplextion: Jesus' apostle Paul said a man was to seek and set his mind on the things that are in Heaven above.* "Whatsoever things are true, whatsoever things are honest, whatsoever things are just, whatsoever things are pure, whatsoever things are lovely, whatsoever things are of good report; if there be any virtue, and if there be any praise, think on these things."*

1) How does one go about apportioning the time spent on the day to day affairs of modern life and the moments dedicated to "higher thinking"?
2) Does the western world spend too much time on the mundane, and too little time thinking of, and aspiring to the Heavenly qualities of life?
3) Generally speaking, does (and /or should) the average man pay any attention to his thoughts and patterns of thinking?

* <u>Bible</u>, Colossians 3:2, (Set your affectation on things above, not on things on the earth.)
** <u>Bible</u>, Philippians 4:8, (... Whatsoever things are lovely, ... think on these things.)

A COIN FLIP

For years I toiled for the side of heads
  From innocence my thoughts were bred
Traditions founded in common law
  But more than one abuse I saw

So alas resigned I would now travail
  For the people's cause, the side of tails
But once again I frowned to see
  A callow show of debauchery

I don't want to be the inquisitor
  Or be caught riding in the getaway car
So if I can my bets I'll hedge
  And play this game from on the edge

A Coin Flip: There's no two ways about it, there are two sides to every story. Searching for the pristine truth, perfect motive, or uncompromising situation in the relative world of nature can be an elusive undertaking. And so perhaps when actions are implicitly in question, it is the character of one's overall intent on which Heaven will ultimately judge.

1) How does one go about deciding which ethical platforms they'll operate from?
2) Does culture, upbringing, and personal experience *always* dictate one's essential moral perspectives?
3) Can a man ever truly avoid "taking moral stands" even when he espouses amoral politics and actively attempts to "stay out of the fray"?

YOU MAKE THE CALL …

Notions of man, troubled in search
    The wisdoms of old on pedestals perch
Simple a time when fall begot fall
    Ponders now he the justice of all
"Mercy" it seems rarely sees light
    The quandary is posed,
What's wrong, and what's right (?)

You Make The Call: The Mosaic law of "an eye for an eye and a tooth for a tooth"* was meant to serve as both a vengeful punishment and a deterrent against future crimes. It is argued that no social system can survive without an orderly code of justice to restrain wrongdoers and maintain a dignified societal standard of human conduct. This said, it is also believed that an "eye for eye" system is wholly lacking as it fails to adequately encourage reformation and does not teach "right actions" to the guilty. Jesus and His fellow proponents of Love and forgiveness instruct mankind to "love your enemies, bless them that curse you, do good to them that hate you, and pray for them that use and persecute you."*

1) Was Jesus saying that criminals should not be punished for their crimes?
2) If, (as many believe) hate, anger and revenge are elements of the evil force in the world, does governmentally sanctioning them serve to reinforce said evil?
3) Can the vibratory force of God's Love, consciously directed by man, neutralize the power of evil?

* <u>Bible</u>, Exodus 21:24, (Eye for an eye, tooth for tooth, hand for hand, foot for foot,)
** <u>Bible</u>, Matthew 5:44, ("But I say unto you, Love your enemies, bless them that curse you, do good to them that hate you, and pray for them which despitefully use you, and persecute you;

CAT-SKINNING FOR PEACE:
THE ENDS AND MEANS ...

Self-willed or fear instilled
    Need they persuade with a gun
        Or with quick-witted pun
           Who shall we blame
                If the outcomes the same ?

Cat-skinning For Peace: Although spiritual laws may be eternally true, there are those who believe their application (as established statutes governing a society) may at different times and ages require modification based on the nature of the environment in which they are enacted. In this thinking, a corrupt and perverse populace, devoid of understanding would be condemned to a system of governance consistent with their level of evolvement, or rather, lack of it.

1) In the present, are there dramatically different legal systems in effect throughout the various countries of the modern world?
2) Are there any measures not currently being exercised that might help reconcile some of the noted differences in geo-political thinking /methods of operation?
3) Ultimately, can a desired outcome really be the same if achieved by different methods? (eg, using force as opposed to diplomacy.)

JUDGED

Complain, complain, they're all insane
And only you, the chosen one
Have sense enough to load the gun ?
Pray be fair I charge of you
For alone you'll stand
When your deeds are through

Judged: The United States of America is often referred to, accused of, and expected to be the "world's policeman". The weighty task of maintaining civil order around the globe is a cumbersome and distasteful undertaking wherein the dictates of sound judgment and practical action are questioned at every turn. However, whether this phenomenon is playing out on a world, country, state, municipal, social, or familial level, collectively, our guide is to mete out judgment with the same measure by which we would prefer to be judged.*

1) Is every man's (nation's) ultimate judgment administered by God and His instruments?*
2) Although Jesus admonished people not to "judge" each other, is there any real escape from societal judgment?*
3) Are those people best qualified to judge (and execute judgments) morally obligated to take-on the task for everyone else's sake?

* Bible, Matthew 7:2, (For with what judgment ye judge, ye shall be judged: and with what measure ye mete, it shall be measured to you again.)
** Bible, Proverbs 29:26, (Many seek the ruler's favor, but every man's judgment cometh from the Lord.)
*** Bible, Matthew 7:1, (Judge not, that ye be not judged.)

PENANCE

A summer night's journey
    The beckoning moon
The fool and his folly
    The madness, the swoon

Were it was quicker
    The night to the day
Would could we alter
    The penance we pay

Penance: Although the sacramental rite of performing "penance" (a repentant act of self-abasement or devotion) to atone for one's sins may be specific in name to certain sects of Christianity, the belief that everyone pays (voluntarily or involuntarily) for their respective crimes against the Universe in the here-and-now and/or in the Hereafter is shared by many of the world religions.

1) Is a man's *every action* preserved /recorded and rewarded appropriately in the Hereafter?*
2) Is there such a thing as "Instant Karma"? (Wherein some acts of goodness or evil are recompensed in the very short run.)
3) Do penitent acts work to absolve one if they are not born of a truly contrite or remorseful spirit?

---

* Koran, Al-Kahf 18:49, (And (on that day) the record (of their deeds) will be exhibited (before them), and you will see those who cut off their ties (with Allah) fearful as to that which is (recorded) in it. They will say, 'Woe to us! What sort of record is this! It leaves out neither a small thing nor a great one but has recounted everything.' And they will find all they did confronting (them) and your Lord does injustice to no one ever.)

FIRE THE SPIRIT

Creatures of habit
    Or habitual creatures
With the carnage abundant
    Where's the spiritual features

In dormant pools
    Of volcanic brew
Laying in silence
    For summons from you?

Fire the Spirit: There are those who believe that "man lies open on one side to the deeps of spiritual nature, to all the attributes of God;" that the mortal physical man is but the organ of his eternal spiritual soul. (R.W. Emerson) To be aware of this truth, coupled with accessing and manifesting this Divine Nature, is the would-be responsible task of all men.

1) Does man have access to all the Divine attributes of his Heavenly Creator?
2) When Jesus said we could do even greater things than He, did he mean we have the innate Godly capacity to create and manifest on a physical plane as well as a spiritual one?
3) How does one go about accessing and making practical use of these God-given gifts and abilities?

* Bible, John 14:12, (Verily, verily I say unto you, He that believeth on me, the works that I do shall he do also; and greater works than these shall he do; because I go unto my Father.)

BOUTONNIERE TACTICS

Peace above victory
The warriors must feign
If for only a moment
From "fighting "again

Scarred but still able
Now wiser, nay brawn
Re-mailed with a flower
As the "war" rages on

Boutonniere Tactics: With the element of human diversity inherently built into the Divine orchestra of global life, it is unreasonable to believe there will be a time, (at least not in any foreseeable future), when the "prevailing public opinion" will be without individual or collective dissent. The methods by which these differing opinions are mediated however is an essential concern of all men. Distancing ourselves from the harsher forms of dispute resolution should be the collective world goal, actively pursued with persistence and imagination.

1) Is it the work of the "righteous" to seek and promote peace?*
2) How successful are the current methods of conflict resolution being used around the world?
3) What other methods might we try to employ on a local, or global level?

* Bible, James 3:18, (And the fruit of righteousness is sown in peace of them that make peace.), Isaiah 32:17, (And the work of righteousness shall be peace; and the effect of righteousness quietness and assurance forever.)

SEDENTARY WAY

With changing tide and warming breeze, The tables turn, he's called to leave
Left behind, a study of life A kaleidoscope of thoughtless strife
The smiles range from glib to snide Unaltered seems the futile stride
Dutiful yield to complacency Securely bogged in apathy

A resting place of wounded wills A burial plot where boredom kills
Feigning desire meets ambitions grave Can doctors cure ? Can heaven save ?
Perhaps the pace is set by Fate A training ground for future great
A milling time around the blocks The pensive wait for the starter's clock

Sedentary Way: "Time" would appear to be frozen in many places on earth. In fact, it would appear an expansive time-line of human experience remains intact amidst the varying pockets of "civilized" and "uncivilized" peoples. The desire to move forward, to break free from ones stagnant circumstance would seem to be a motivating stimulus for many in all parts of the world. However, the limited ready opportunities to do so sap the strength, and quell the impetus needed to escape the accustomed ruts of standard routine. The result is a general social malaise, and a systemic continued quashing of would-be progress.

1) Have recent technological advances reduced some of the disparities in these areas?
2) What International Development Programs could be formed and implemented to accommodate this collective inherent initiative?
3) Given the general nature of the workings of the world at large (as we currently know it), will it ever be possible for the global populace to be on the "same page" socially, politically, and/or technologically?

MEMORY

And when it seems no longer
Worthy of the pain
The memory just grows stronger
As you step onto the plane

And perhaps another rainbow
Will one day fill your sky
Perhaps the sun tomorrow
Will shine on how and why

Memory: There would seem to be a countless array of causes that leave men with unpleasant memories. These troublesome thoughts, feelings, and experiences can steal the light from ones otherwise acceptable life. The release of this acute or chronic inner grief is the subject addressed and objective sought by many a patient and parishioner alike. However, whether on a personal or group level, the ability to attain emotional closure regarding these matters is often a daunting task.

1) Although it doesn't always work, are there times when changing ones personal venue can actually help ease inner burdens?
2) Besides psychotherapy and prayer, what are some other methods or tools used to successfully achieve emotional convalescence, closure, and/or peace of mind?
3) Does all "real change" of one's mental or emotional state come from "within"?

SEDUCTION

Candles yearn, desires burn
Dim the lights to low
Another glass of wine? you ask
As the bubbles take their toll

Alas the prey is nicely put
Wrapped in passions glow
The lure of Love, the dance on earth
The "high" both long to know

As we live and breathe the fantasy
Pray be fair our fates to fall
For the call of Aphrodite
Seduces one and all

Seduction: People are seduced by a variety of things: beauty, wealth, power, fame. But it's arguably Love that holds the greatest sway over man. It is the much sought after, and often most elusive sacred fruit. And so, in a traditional culture, underpinned with the precepts of guarded chastity and shackled by the limitations of pecuniary solvency, it is perhaps understandable, if not forgivable, when the promise of Love is used as the inducement to gain access to a possessor's charms or riches.

1) Can one be tempted into doing anything that they do not already have an inclination, predisposition or desire to do?
2) Under what circumstances, if any, is it morally acceptable to induce one towards disloyalty, disobedience, or impropriety by means of persuasion or false promises?
3) Presuming no disingenuous intention, can the arts of seduction lead to happy endings?

REGRET

Maybe you never should have loved them
Did you only make them cry ?
The human heart is fragile
And the hope for Love is high

Regret: It is said that the greatest Love is an unrequited Love. It is also said that it is better to have loved and lost than to never have loved at all. For some, the pain of Love momentarily found and then lost is a harmful burden to bear. And thus it's tricky business, even if the original sentiment is honorable and true, when dabbling in the confines of ephemeral rapture, risking the well-being of those unbeknownst delicate souls.

1) Are there recognizable characteristics of a fragile emotional nature?
2) Can a short-lived romantic tryst really be honorable?
3) What role does amative discretion play in a civilized society?

NEON AMOUR

City lights, neon lights, desert, earth and sea
    They come from where it's everybody
All look the same to me

Luscious lips, and fingertips, a painted jezebel
    And now I'm lost in my euphoria
Weak underneath her spell

You play the game, you feel the shame
    A shadow's in the hall
Another love, with embers dying
    Bet you can't name them all

And then you fall, wizen up
    Can't you see the hole ?
If you are sure, the time is ready
    Ease into "The Role"

Neon Amour: The Holy books of this world are flush with scriptures admonishing us to refrain from diving into the pool of temporal delights; to resist the temptations found in amorous affairs and carnal passions. And yet it would seem in many circles these cautionary tales are left unheeded. Rather, practical experience is promoted, even encouraged, up to the point where personal circumstance reveals the veracity of the heretofore noted divinatory advice.

1) Are the traditional sexual mores of modern culture antiquated or out-dated?
2) How much of our societal dictates in these areas is founded in practically?
3) Does the sowing of one's "wild oats" during their youth have any practical applications?

EPILEPSY

Brain waves roll, nerves astray
A synapse or two along the way

Fade away to "channel one"
Petimal cool, the trips begun

A soul cries out, the Grandmal stir
Will calm prevail, or death occur

Epilepsy: The abnormal electrical discharges in the brain associated with epilepsy come in degrees of severity and duration. Review of case studies reveals that some sufferers apparently have the ability to sense an episode developing and can either quash it or let it occur. There are those who believe this phenomenon parallels man's innate abilities to heal himself, or conversely, make himself ill. These intrinsic aptitudes are thought to be in direct association with ones conscious, and more acutely, subconscious beliefs.

1) When Jesus said, "... Physician, heal thyself:"* was he also speaking to *man's* physical ability to do just that?
2) Are psychosomatic illnesses and spontaneous healings on the opposite ends of the same causality spectrum?
3) How closely does one's physical health follow their emotional and/or psychological expectations?

* Bible, Luke 4:23, (And he said to them, "Ye will surely say unto me this proverb, Physician, heal thyself: ...)

THIS IS A TEST

Is this the only one ?
　　　The height of some ?
The low of most ?

Or another proving ground
　　　With Gods renowned
And the Holy Ghost (?)

This is a Test: Whether one believes they live only one life on Earth, or are reincarnated repeatedly to live many lives, it would seem that each life has its lessons to be learned. It is said that identifying one's purpose in life, (be it specific or general in nature) is paramount to living a fulfilled existence, and successfully advancing the progress of the soul. Guidance in these areas is said to be provided by the beneficent Universal Intelligences in response to simple requests for the same.

1) If this is everyone's only life on Earth, why would there be such disparities in the health, wealth, position and general quality of life between given individuals?
2) If people believed they had many life times to reach their goal of soul perfection, would it necessarily diminish their efforts in their present life?
3) Is the Holy Ghost or Holy Spirit an eternal element of God Himself, ever accessible to mankind via earnest petition?

BY THE BY

By the left
    By the right
By the way
    By the might
By the love
    By the fright
By the by
    God is Light ...
        and Amore.

By the By: The enigmatic nature of God and His creation continually baffles the rational minds of men. Our limited faculties of reason would appear insufficient to comprehend the motives of the Beginningless and Uncaused. And so, perhaps by design, it is the spiritual intuition of His devotees upon which we rely for glimpses of His essence and intent. Both Vedic and Biblical teachings advise that God is Light*, and Love;** that His very nature is Bliss, and that a man in attunement with Him experiences boundless joy.

1) With respect to life on Earth, is it each man's active duty to attempt to discern God's intent and wishes?
2) Is it presumptuous to think there is only one "way" to serve and /or seek union with God?
3) Does God want mankind to be joyful?, to live in a state of happiness, fulfillment and bliss?***

---

* Bible, I John 1:5, (This then is the message which we have heard of Him, and declare unto you, that God is light, and in Him is no darkness at all.)
** Bible, I John 4:8, (He that loveth not knoweth not God; for God is Love.)
*** Bible, ("Fear not, little flock; for it is your Father's good pleasure to give you the kingdom.")

PARALYZED

Real or imagined, the maya of all,
Cosmic illusion, the invisible wall
Strangled by shadows, tethered with myth,
The soul seeks its freedom from the internal abyss

The deafening drone of the ego let loose,
The gallows of man, his unrecognized noose
Pray search the within for ponderous truth,
Pray shackle the darkness for luminous views

The Good or the evil, the choice facing all,
Though avoiding the riddle man continues to crawl
Babes in the darkness, alone and afraid,
To even venture an answer to the riddle self made

Paralyzed: Proponents and practitioners of transcendental self-actualization methods advise that man, inherently imbued with an immortal soul, is largely blind to this fact as a result of the delusive nature of the "physical" world. Efforts to realize ones true spiritual nature can be accomplished through yoga-style meditations, where direct contact and (re)union with the Divine elements is the objective. It is believed that many spiritual masters, prophets, sages, yogis, and the like were, and are, in tune with these Cosmic channels. To transcend the madness of the world, mankind, as the primary directive, has only to seek God and His direction through these means.

1) Does the first of the Biblical Ten Commandments, "Thou shalt have no other gods before me"* support the belief that man should seek and serve God first and foremost?

2) Did Jesus affirm this Heavenly mandate when he said we should love God with all of our heart, mind, soul and strength, as the first commandment?**

3) Does His admonition to allay any concerns about material well-being, and to ... "seek ye the kingdom of God, and all these things will be added unto you"*** leave any doubt about His belief?

* Bible, Exodus 20:3, Deuteronomy 5:7, (Thou shalt have no other gods before Me.)
** Bible, Mark 12:30, ("And thou shalt love the Lord thy God with all thy heart, and with all thy soul, and with all the mind, and with all thy strength: this is the first commandment.") (See also Matthew 22:37)
*** Bible, Luke 12:31, ("But rather seek ye the kingdom of God: and all these things shall be added unto you."

COME TOGETHER

A money back guarantee
The only place for you and me
Come black come white come all to see
The comfort found in unity

Come Together: The belief in and application of the inalienable rights of all men is the stalwart codified benchmark against which all nations should measure their standards and progress. And though admittedly imperfect, it should be with pride and a sense of communal purpose that we stand shoulder to shoulder as a multi-cultural assembly, bearing daily witness to the Providential power of the unified diverse. May our collective efforts in this regard be Heavenly blessed.

1) Is it by accident, or Divine fate that the United States of America is the world's melting pot; the sought after hallowed ground, perennially drawing to it the myriad masses?
2) Do we have a unique obligation to actively exemplify the enviable qualities of mutual respect and appreciation for our varied ethnicities, conventions and customs?
3) By what means do men evolve from a mere tolerance of different philosophies and practices to a deferential regard?

3RD WORLD RESCUE

They never go nowhere, they got nothing to do
They're bored, very, very bored.
So I think it's time we give them a job
Give them a chance, don't *make* them rob
No one *wants* to be bored

Dig it. Like I was watching TV the other night
It was PBS and oh what a sight
I saw kwashiorkor babies with their bellies abloat
'Cause they got no McDoanlds and they got no Coke
They live in little grass huts with no windows or doors
While my pappies in the kitchen eating some more
Oh no!, some more ?!

Well I think we need the army's core of engineers
To trade all weapons for construction gear
We'll train the nukes, the dukes
The bloods and the crips
Give 'em all hammers, backhoes and picks
We'll build some shelters, dig some wells
Hand out baby blankets, and oh what the hell
Lets do strip malls, let's give 'em it all

They need a 7-11 there in the middle of hell
A Chucky Cheese pizza and Taco Bell
Sears and Starbucks, Chevrolet
Come on people let's get started today
We'll do a revamp. No more death camp.

They need indoor plumbing, paneled walls
Electric lights and shower stalls
Irrigated deserts, Skippy on the shelf
It just won't pay to leave it clay
Let's proceed with global health

So come on down, sign on the line
Give us say, a year of your time
Get on the payroll, meet Alejandro
It's no sweat bro, come home a hero
We'll do a remake, we'll have a clam bake
We'll build a new world, no more 3rd world
When we help them, we help ourselves, So let's do it. Get to it.

3rd World Rescue: Though it's not new thinking, it's nice to know there are modern geopolitical policy advisers and futurologists who support the belief that the only real way to assure peace and prosperity on a global scale is to systematically strive to narrow the gap between the "haves" and the "have-nots". This of course makes perfect sense as we all remember the lessons we learned in the school yard when we were kids: that is, people as a rule become disgruntled when they're excluded from "the game". And the game in this case is the opportunity to share in a reasonable facsimile of economic parity.

1) Albeit there are high hurdles associated with manifesting these ideals, is the continued endeavor to do so anything other than en-lighten self-interest?
2) What measures would have to be employed to initiate F.D.R.'s "New Deal" type programs on an international level?
3) Given the fascist and dictatorial nature of many existing national re-gimes is it realistic to believe that comprehensive social and eco-nomic progress can be achieved (at least any time soon) without an element of military interdiction?

UNITED

Don't be deceived, warnings he read
To follow a path to sorrow it led
Notions of truth, ideas of old
The road of the fool, the way of the bold
Caution it seems thrown to the wind
Deep are the waters and long is the swim
"Faithless" he cries as saddened he falls
One less foothold in climbing the wall
Narrow it's said the way of the true
Direction is found to those who pursue
Many still find the answers a mist
Blinded are those who claim earthly bliss ?
Brothers in straights, sisters in hell
From ages to pages their history befell
Around and about the postures of time
Grandeur was his now grandeur is mine
The questions are old, ancient the lies
Eden on earth the heaven they buy
The weak and the dark, the light of the new
To cast away shadows, to choose but a few ?
Mysteries of thought, follies so called
The power within, the conscience of all
Pedestals high we teeter upon
But only from oneness will night beget dawn

United: United we stand. Divided we fall. "And if a kingdom be divided against itself, that kingdom cannot stand. And if a house be divided against itself, that house cannot stand."* With each passing moment the world becomes more and more a global community, and as such, we are incrementally compelled to expand our views and embrace our new neighbors. And although isolationistic thinking is still pretty easy to find around town, it appears highly unlikely that Providence intends to turn back the clock.

1) With the axiom "fences make good neighbors" considered, what level of cohesive togetherness should we expect and attempt to achieve in the short term?
2) Can we use interfaith and rainbow coalition type groups as templates for establishing the dialogue and forming the new paradigms that will be required to successfully meld diverse philosophic and religious perspectives?
3) Within what time frame is a one-world federation of countries an actual achievable goal?

* <u>Bible</u>, Mark 3:24-25, ("And if a kingdom be divided against itself, that kingdom cannot stand. And if a house be divided against itself, that house cannot stand.")

FINNY

I watch the rocks
I drift along
The river's edge
From dusk 'til dawn
The eddy's course
Has been my song
The rueful turns
Of a trail forlong
I see by suns
Of midnight sky
By lunar glint
In cautious eyes
Far destiny
Can know not I
My trust I place
In Fate's Ally

Finny: There is many a lonesome soul, drifting, aimless, orphaned by the time and circumstance of life. And even though Fate would appear to have dealt them a losing hand, its Author is ever available for those who in Him would abide. "The Lord is good, a strong hold in the day of trouble; and He knoweth them that trust in Him."*

1) Is a "fated" outcome synonymous with a "destined" outcome?
2) Does "blind chance" play any part in one's fate or destiny?
3) Are there quantifiable determining wills, principles or causes behind someone's fate?

* <u>Bible</u>, Nahum 1:7, (The Lord is good, a stronghold in the day of trouble; and he knoweth them that trust in Him.)

ASSUMPTION

Mary Lou and sister Sue
Took a trip to score
A bag of herbs for brother Merv
At Callie's health food store

The door was open
But alas they found
No one to ring the sale
So they took the stash
And left the cash
On the counter by the scale

Their intent was good
But fate this time
Would be of fickle kind
For Callie saw the missing herbs
But never came to find
The meager fare of the lady pair
So quickly she did call
Officer Dan and his best man
Lieutenant Ingersol

The boys set out to solve the case
And lo the two discovered
The girls enroute to Mervin's house
And the "crime" it was uncovered
The herbs they found in Mary's bag
And now our friend we see
Growing old, but ever bold
In the jail of destiny

Assumption: The variable probabilities inherent in the principles of risk assumption are the concerns of all who foray into ventures of a speculative nature; (wherein the possibility of loss exists). These arenas are broad in scope, and on some corollary level touch virtually every aspect of human endeavor. It would be said that every form of loss has its negative or unfortunate component. However it is loss resulting from perils unrecognized or underappreciated that are the hardest to bear.

1) Are the outcomes of events always predictable (within given parameters) and subject to simple statistics of a fixed nature (probability distribution functions)?
2) Are there employable factors, practices or influences available to annul, override or otherwise usurp the results of a customary or expected outcome?
3) Is it possible to modulate, minimize, or eliminate typical physical exposures with or by metaphysical inter-session?

POLLUNTANYS

**Poisoned by the air we breathe
Poisoned by the tales they weave
Poisoned by the "will of Eve"
Poisoned 'til the day we leave**

Polluntanys: Reconciling the contradictory aspects of Nature would seem to many the impossible mission, as He who made puppies put snakes in the grass. However, there is some belief that the world was not always dichotomous, that *mankind's* "fall from grace" precipitated a dastardly negative impact on the qualities of plants (and perhaps animals) as well.* And so maybe Earth itself *was* once a veritable Garden of Eden of peace and tranquility, and may again be someday.** For now though, it would seem we make our way under the decidedly duplicitous cast of an at once benevolent and angry Sun.

1) What does it mean in the Bible when it says that man was created in God's image?***
2) Using the miracles of Jesus, and other recorded yogic masters as examples, does the highly evolved man truly have dominion over the elements of the physical world?
3) Could a progressive change in the mass collective conscious of mankind trigger a parallel phase transition in the world of plants and animals? (wild to tame, as it were).

* Bible, Genesis 4:17, 18, ("And unto Adam He said, ... cursed is the ground for thy sake; in sorrow shalt thou eat of it all the days of your life; thorns also and thistles shall it bring forth to thee; and thou shalt eat the herb of the field;")
** Bible, Isaiah 11:6-9, (The wolf also shall dwell with the lamb, and the leopard shall lie down with the kid; and the calf and the young lion and the fatling together; and a little child shall lead them. ... .)
*** Bible, Genesis 1:26, 27, (And God said , let us make man in our image, after our likeness: and let them have dominion over the fish of the sea, and over the fowl of the air, and over the cattle, and over all the earth, and over every creeping thing that creepeth upon the earth. And so God created man in His own image, in the image of God created He him; male and female created He them.

FOLLY

Loudly at times, though softly more still
The voices of folly, do beckon my will

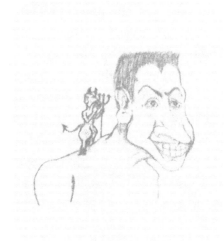

Folly: "Now the serpent was more subtle than any beast of the field which the Lord God had made."* It is widely held that the serpent in the Biblical story about Eve and the Garden of Eden is a metaphor for the devil, or the miasmic, defiling forces which are said to incessantly assail the reason of men. And many would say it is the fool who lowers his guard, abandons his ideals, and surrenders his will to those would-be purveyors of ignorant lusts.

1) Is it possible for a man to control all his thoughts in the same fashion as he controls his actions?
2) Is it "promiscuous" to allow one's thoughts to dwell on the malevolent, wicked or depraved?
3) Are one's thoughts a physical form of energy, for better or worse?

* Bible, Genesis 3:1, ("Now the serpent was more subtle than any beast of the field which the Lord God had made.")

DIAL "D" FOR ...

I called to see what scandal played
On today's "Record a Wrong"
The message said we're out for now
But won't be gone for long
You see you've dialed LOgan 8
Seven Fifty-two
We are the gossip monger
And we've got the dirt for you

So I waited twenty minutes
And called them back again
This time a voice said, "Mornin' Love,
Shall we let the show begin ?"

"Well Billy Ray is still in heels
And combs his hair with mud
Molly Bent can't pay the rent
So lives on booze and bud

Doctor Fee and General Lee
Still fight the bloody wars
Over fetal rights, and megabytes
To give, or take some more

And preacher Dan he has a plan
To save us all from heck
But the price is always higher
Than the limit on your check

And it's true the sun tomorrow
Will make you squint your eyes
And the swill you ate for dinner
Will settle in your thighs

And we all know that life is fatal
But to ourselves we'll lie
We all want to go to Heaven
But no one wants to die."

Beeep !
"Your dime has now expired. My how time has flown.
So now do yourself a favor, and hang-up at the tone.
rrrrrr .....

Dial "D" for ... One certainly doesn't have to look very long or far to see what's "wrong" with the world. The daily news is filled with the latest scandal, disaster, and tragedy. And folks argue about whether the world is mostly good, or mostly bad. But as long as it's the *bad* news making headlines, perhaps that means on the whole it's the anomaly and not the norm.

1) How is it people seem to have such a penchant for bad news?
2) Is it a ghoulish propensity that causes a man to slow down and gawk at the train wreck?
3) Does man's inherent compassion and empathy also spur him to express and pay attention to "misfortune", and the unfortunate?

AND THE LORD SAID ...

And the Lord said,

> "Vengeance is mine ...",
>> So seemingly clear
> Why then Nature's repine,
>> As the calm to our fears
> Suspect are all,
>> Imperfect and weak
> Pray be you absolved,
>> When for the Faultless you speak

And the Lord Said ...: The Holy Koran would seem to encourages men toward forgiveness when it says that we may have the right to seek equitable justice for injuries suffered, but would secure an expiation (forgiveness) of our own sins should we choose to forego the demand for revenge. * Jesus' Apostle Paul said, "Dearly beloved, avenge not yourselves, but rather give place unto wrath: for it is written, Vengeance is Mine; I will repay, saith the Lord."**

It would be nice if the world came replete with a system of "*Instant Karma*" wherein justice in its varied forms was automatically implemented to the appeasement and satisfaction of its citizens. And though this at times does occur, it is not generally the case. As such, the burden of attempting to impose a "pure justice" is left to the designs and devices of mankind, the inherently "impure judge".

1) On a personal level, is it better to let the Universe "even the score" when subjected to affronts of a lesser nature?
2) And further, didn't Jesus advise us to actually pray for our tormentor's forgiveness (with the knowing understanding that their

"crimes" would inevitably come around full circle to harm them as well?).***

3) Is there a point after which a pious, conscientious man should (can) no longer "turn the other cheek"?****

---

* Koran, Al-Maidah 5:45, (And therein We laid down (the following law) for them (- the Jews); life for life and eye for eye, and nose for nose an ear for ear and tooth for tooth and for (other) injuries an equitable retaliation. But he who chooses to forego (the right) thereto for the sake of Allah, it shall be an expiation (*forgiveness*) of sins for him. ...)

** Bible, Romans 12:19, (Dearly beloved, avenge not yourselves, but rather give place to wrath: for it is written, Vengeance is mine; I will repay, saith the Lord.)

*** Bible, Luke 23:34, (Then said Jesus, "Father, forgive them, for they know not what they do.")

**** Bible, Matthew 5:39, ("But I say unto you, That ye resist not evil: but whosoever shall smite thee on thy right cheek, turn to him the other also.)

NEW WORLD TWIST

It's a change of age so turn the page
We've all seen this bilge before
It's time to reach and stretch ourselves
For peace is at our door
Who says we have to die enmasse
In squalor and in pain
We've all got the stuff to make this trip
Without the sweat and strain
A simple man in modern times
Knows enough to make it fine
So just flex your wrist and flip the disc
And get on down with the new world twist

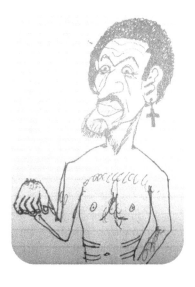

New World Twist: In equal measure mankind is afforded the daily opportunity to operate from platforms of Love and compassion, or distain and neglect. And while some fatalistic elements of western culture predict and expect an apocalyptic end of the world as we know it, this sentiment and expectation is not shared by other world beliefs. Some expect that it will be through the active expression of the Buddha, Christ, Krishna, or God-consciousness within mankind as a whole that ultimately establishes God's Kingdom of Heaven here on Earth. Regardless of one's personal perspective, soliciting this Godly Spirit, and manifesting It's Heavenly Fruit in the here and now would seem our individual and collective mission, this day, and every day.

1) Could the fall of Babylon, as recorded in the Bible's Book of Revelation, be a metaphorical warning for all City-states /empires that forsake the precepts of righteousness for the wanton pursuit of material and sensual gratifications?
2) Since the above-noted writings of St. John the Divine were first inscribed have there been numerous apocalyptic destructions of secular empires?
3) In the writings of the Old Testament prophets, are there examples of City-states that heeded their spiritual warnings and were spared the cataclysmic destiny of their previous ways?*

* Bible, Jonah 3:4-10, (... So the people of Nineveh believed God, and proclaimed a fast, and put on sackcloth, from the greatest of them even to the least of them. ... And God saw their works, that they turned from their evil way; and God repented of the evil, that He had said that He would do unto them; and He did it not.)

NEWTON'S LAW

I once saw a man suspended in air
Bald as an apple with nare a hair
T'was a mystery to me what kept him afloat
For I saw not a wire, a cable or rope

Now I'd read about yogis who hovered upon
Invisible beds of excited Ergone
Or some kind of "gas" of cosmic design
To witness the power of a spirit divine

So right up I walked and ventured to ask
In what bed of waves did the good fellow bask ?
He smiled a smile much wryer than bread
Opened an eye and then casually said

"On pillows of wisdom do I rest my lot
On lore of the mystics long since forgot
On secrets of gods to men rarely shown
But a riddle there isn't that wasn't once known

The trick is to bury the ego in Love
And serve not the self but the Heavens above
When yours is the will of The Masters of Time
Gravitation becomes but a state of the mind."

Newton's Law: Although the good Lord may have supplanted us in a mysterious and ever-evolving creation, He also imparted in us the desire and ability to question and understand. And it may be the wont of the secular West to explain the "miracles" of the metaphysical in terrestrial terms, it is believed their rational approach will one day reveal the transcendental truths of which the enlightened East claim an intimate knowledge. Our continued earnest quest for the emancipation of these heavenly verities brings us each day closer to their realization.

1) Are there different "planes of reality" that can and do co-exist simultaneously on Earth? (ie, is it actually possible to suspend, or operate beyond the natural laws of physics as we know them.)

2) Are spontaneous healings, and the abilities associated with extra-sensory perception (ESP), such as clairvoyance and telekinesis, examples of known phenomena which do just that?

3) Are there simple, straight-forward, practical means and methods (such as prayer and meditation) that can elevate one from a lower to higher plane of operation?

LIGHT YEARS

I wonder where I'll be, let's say
A million years from yesterday
I wonder if I'll still be "me"
In a kind of parallel galaxy
I think a "heaven" place would do me well
Somewheres a year or two from hell.
Light years that is.

Light Years: The permanency of the human soul leads us to wonder and speculate as the nature and circumstance of its future state. The possibility of maintaining ones tactile and/or conscious awareness in the hereafter compels all to hope for the eventuality of a euphoric condition. And in many cases, it is fear of the polar opposite that drives men down the road of moral and ethical propriety.

1) Can ones wicked actions in this life cause them to "lose" their soul forever?; (ie, is there any crime against the Universe that is unforgivable?)
2) Do all souls have the possibility of redemption, albeit some may have a longer way to go than others?
3) Could /would God create a circumstantial world wherein a part of Himself could be permanently "lost"?

DRAWING BOARDS

With empathy hone
Your futile scheme
With wisdom mold
Your ragged dream
Refine your wreckage
With calloused hand
And resign your will
To understand

Drawing Boards: Tempestuous winds of change blow in a widening arc across the span of humanity, challenging all to reconcile, adjust, and adapt. The shifting paradigms of global interaction will require the inspired formulation and steady application of new and resourceful socio-political and socio-economic strategies. Successfully accommodating the disparate agendas of our present multi-polar era will not occur overnight, nor will it happen without a dedicated communal effort.

1) Are there current national and/or international organizations that are in need of transformation, transfiguration, or metamorphosis? (eg, US State Department, World Trade Organization, World Bank, etc)
2) What new domestic and/or multi-national organizations should be formed in the interest of promoting universal progress?
3) What role could /should private non-governmental organizations play in the grand scheme of things?

UTOPIA COMES

On a moonlit path under midnight skies
    Apprehension filled his amber eyes
For reason strained to find allies
    While madness lurked in thin disguise

But birthed an age and changed did tide
    The tempest quelled by open eyes
Now duty serves where once did hide
    And king to pawn travail in stride.

Utopia Comes: History has seen no shortage of poets, visionaries, philosophers and conceptualists who have espoused this or that version of an idyllic utopian society. Once considered though, the diverse range of ideas from Plato to Thomas More unceremoniously underscores the reality that one man's heaven doesn't always match-up with another's. As such, some would label efforts to move our multi-cultural realities toward a universal synthesis of co-existent bliss as absurd, foolhardy, and naïve. And of course, in one sense at least, they are right.

It is however within our collective abilities to maintain, extend, and improve our awareness, recognition, and understanding of the various social, civic, and economic components that comprise the modern tapestry of our respective belief systems, structures and institutions. And though admittedly besot with future failures and embarrassments, it is a fluid, optimistic, inspired effort that will ultimately illuminate the simple metaphysical principles on which a peaceful and harmonious world will be built. To that eventuality, let us all strive.

1) Truth be told, do people's desires and expectations of a "heavenly" existence vary all that much?
2) What things, beyond the Love of family, respect of peers, material comforts, and freedom from pain and misery, do folks actually want?
3) Is any heavenly actuality available without the overwhelming influence of God, Goodness and Love?

POSTSCRIPT

Domesticating Earth's wildest species: Man

With obvious, noteworthy, and thankful exception, the whole of mankind has yet to be tamed. This unfortunate phenomenon is all too evident as for after thousands of years man continues his intra-species assault in brutal fashion.

And yet, as the butterfly by destiny transforms the larvae, man too is endowed with a naturally ambitious spirit. He is ever mindful and wantonly compelled to manifest this inherently providential element. 'Tis folly that we allow this urge, this desire, this calling to lay dormant, to languish obscured. Rather should we actively accommodate this yearning, embraced and nurtured so to realize its fullest potential.

Let us to a man transform the beast within while we can still call Earth our home, and accept now our rightfully fated sovereignty as the theomorphic entities we know ourselves to be.

"The essential component of all legitimate religions and philosophies is about Sharing, Caring, Giving and spreading Love.

Let your Love light shine so brightly that others can find their way out of darkness.

'The heights of great men, reached and kept,
Were not attained by sudden flight.
But they, while their companions slept,
Were toiling upward in the night.'*

'One Love. One Heart. Let's get together and feel alright.' **

Amen brother."

HAROLD

*Henry Wadsworth Longfellow, (American Poet; 27 February 1807 to 24 March 1882), excerpt from *The Ladder of St. Augustine*, (1858).

**Bob Nesta Marley, (Jamaican singer, song writer and musician; 6 February 1945 to 11 May 1981), excerpt from song lyric One Love/People Get Ready

FOOTNOTES

All referenced footnotes are from the King James Version of <u>The Holy Bible</u>, except **Uh, Waiting for Hell?**, page 81, **Penance**, page 98, and **And the Lord Said …**, page 120 which are from the Allamah Nooruddin rendering of <u>The Holy Quran (Koran)</u>.

1. **Faith**, page 6, <u>Bible</u>; Matthew 17:20 & Mark 12:22-23, (" … for verily I say unto you, if ye have faith as a grain of mustard seed, ye shall say unto this mountain, remove hence to yonder place, and it shall remove; …")
2. **Faith,** page 6, <u>Bible</u>; Matthew 7:7, (Ask, and it shall be given you; seek, and ye shall find; knock, and it shall be opened unto you.)
3. **Duty**, page 18, <u>Bible</u>; Genesis 3: 1-24, (… Therefore the Lord God sent him forth from the garden of Eden, to till the ground from whence he was taken. …)
4. **The Innocent Ones**, page 20, <u>Bible</u>; Genesis 9:1, (And God blessed Noah and his sons, and said unto them, "Be fruitful, and multiply, and replenish the Earth.")
5. **Unity Via Continuum**, page 26, <u>Bible</u>; Acts 17:26, (And (God) hath made of one blood all nations of men for to dwell on all the face of the Earth;").
6. **Derision**, Page 33, <u>Bible</u>; Mark 7: 18-20, (" … whatsoever thing from without entereth into the man, it cannot defile him; … that which cometh out of the man, that defileth the man.")
7. **Bow**, page 39, <u>Bible</u>; Matthew 16: 25, ("For whosoever will save his life shall lose it: …")
8. **Capital Justice**, page 39, <u>Bible</u>; Matthew 5:39, (" But I say unto you, that ye resist not evil; but whosoever shall smite you thee on the right cheek, turn to him the left cheek also.")
9. **Capital Justice**, page 39, <u>Bible</u>; Matthew 26:52, (Then Jesus said unto him, "Put up again thy sword into his place; for all they that take the sword shall perish with the sword.")

10. **Make a Move**, page 66, <u>Bible</u>; John 14:12, ("Verily, verily, I say unto you, He that believeth on me, the works that I do shall he do also; and greater *works* than these shall he do; because I go unto my Father.")
11. **Carpe Diem**, page 67, <u>Bible</u>; Matthew 6:25-34, (" Therefore I say unto you, take no thought for your life, what you shall eat, or what ye shall drink, ... Take therefore no thought for the morrow; for the morrow shall take thought for the things of itself. ...")
12. **So Long**, page 74, <u>Bible</u>; Matthew 5:4, ("Blessed are they that mourn: for they shall be comforted.")
13. **So Long**, page 74, <u>Bible</u>; Galatians 6:9, (And let us not be weary in well doing: for in due season we will reap, if we faint not.)
14. **Uh, waiting for Hell?**, page 84, <u>Koran</u>: Fussilat 41:46, (He that does right, does it for the good of his own soul, and he that does evil, it shall recoil on him.)
15. **Brass Rings**, page 89, <u>Bible</u>, Luke 12:32, (Fear not, little flock, for it is your Father's good pleasure to give you the kingdom.)
16. **Mammon**, page 90, <u>Bible</u>, Matthew 6:24, (No man can serve two masters; for either he will hate the one, and love the other; or else he will hold to one, and despise the other. Ye cannot serve God and mammon.)
17. **See the Light**, page 94, <u>Bible</u>, Ecclesiastes 3:1, (To everything there is a season, and a time to every purpose under the heaven;)
18. **Patience**, page 95, <u>Bible</u>, Luke 8:15, (But that on the good ground are they, which in an honest and good heart, having heard the word, keep *it*, and bring forth fruit with patience.)
19. **Poet's Perplextion**, page 97, <u>Bible</u>, Colossians 3:2, (Set your affectation on things above, not on things on the earth.)
20. **Poet's Perplextion**, page 97, <u>Bible</u>, Philippians 4:8, (... Whatsoever things are lovely, ... think on these things.)
21. **You Make the Call**, page 99, <u>Bible</u>, Exodus 21:24, (Eye for an eye, tooth for tooth, hand for hand, foot for foot,)
22. **You Make the Call**, page 99, <u>Bible</u>, Matthew 5:44, ("But I say unto you, Love your enemies, bless them that curse you, do good to them that hate you, and pray for them which despitefully use you, and persecute you;")

23. **Judged**, page 101, <u>Bible</u>, Matthew 7:2, (For with what judgment ye judge, ye shall be judged: and with what measure ye mete, it shall be measured to you again.)
24. **Judged**, page 101, <u>Bible</u>, Proverbs 29:26, (Many seek the ruler's favor, but every man's judgment cometh from the Lord.)
25. **Judged**, page 101, <u>Bible</u>, Matthew 7:1, (Judge not, that ye be not judged.)
26. **Penance**, page 102, <u>Koran</u>, Al-Kahf 18:49, (And (on that day) the record (of their deeds) will be exhibited (before them), and you will see those who cut off their ties (with Allah) fearful as to that which is (recorded) in it. They will say, 'Woe to us! What sort of record is this! It leaves out neither a small thing nor a great one but has recounted everything.' And they will find all they did confronting (them) and your Lord does injustice to no one ever.)
27. **Boutonniere Tactics**, page 104, <u>Bible</u>, James 3:18, (And the fruit of righteousness is sown in peace of them that make peace.), Isaiah 32:17, (And the work of righteousness shall be peace; and the effect of righteousness quietness and assurance forever.)
28. **Epilepsy**, page 110, <u>Bible</u>, Luke 4:23, (And he said to them, "Ye will surely say unto me this proverb, Physician, heal thyself: ...)
29. **Paralyzed**, page 113, <u>Bible</u>, Exodus 20:3, Deuteronomy 5:7, (Thou shalt have no other gods before Me.)
30. **Paralyzed**, page 113, <u>Bible</u>, Mark 12:30, ("And thou shalt love the Lord thy God with all thy heart, and with all thy soul, and with all thy mind, and with all thy strength: this is the first commandment.") (See also Matthew 22:37)
31. **Paralyzed**, page 113, <u>Bible</u>, Luke 12:31, ("But rather seek ye the kingdom of God: and all these things shall be added unto you.")
32. **By the By**, page 112, <u>Bible</u>, I John 1:5, (This then is the message which we have heard of Him, and declare unto you, that God is light, and in Him is no darkness at all.)
33. **By the By**, page 112, <u>Bible</u>, I John 4:8, (He that loveth not knoweth not God; for God is Love.)
34. **By the By**, page 112, <u>Bible</u>, ("Fear not, little flock; for it is your Father's good pleasure to give you the kingdom.")

35. **United**, page 118, <u>Bible</u>, Mark 3:24-25, ("And if a kingdom be divided against itself, that kingdom cannot stand. And if a house be divided against itself, that house cannot stand.")

36. **Finny**, page 120, <u>Bible</u>, Nahum 1:7, (The Lord is good, a stronghold in the day of trouble; and he knoweth them that trust in Him.)

37. **Pollutanys**, page 123, <u>Bible</u>, Genesis 4:17, 18, ("And unto Adam He said, ... cursed is the ground for thy sake; in sorrow shalt thou eat of it all the days of your life; thorns also and thistles shall it bring forth to thee; and thou shalt eat the herb of the field;")

38. **Pollutanys**, page 123, <u>Bible</u>, Isaiah 11:6-9, (The wolf also shall dwell with the lamb, and the leopard shall lie down with the kid; and the calf and the young lion and the fatling together; and a little child shall lead them. ... .)

39. **Pollutanys**, page 123, <u>Bible</u>, Genesis 1:26, 27, (And God said , let us make man in our image, after our likeness: and let them have dominion over the fish of the sea, and over the fowl of the air, and over the cattle, and over all the earth, and over every creeping thing that creepeth upon the earth. And so God created man in His own image, in the image of God created He him; male and female created He them.)

40. **Folly,** page 124, <u>Bible,</u> Genesis 3:1, ("Now the serpent was more subtle than any beast of the field which the Lord God had made.")

41. **And the Lord said ...**, page 127, <u>Koran</u>, Al-Maidah 5:45, (And therein We laid down (the following law) for them (- the Jews); life for life and eye for eye, and nose for nose an ear for ear and tooth for tooth and for (other) injuries an equitable retaliation. But he who chooses to forego (the right) thereto for the sake of Allah, it shall be an expiation (*forgiveness*) of sins for him. ...)

42. **And the Lord said ...**, page 127, <u>Bible</u>, Romans 12:19, (Dearly beloved, avenge not yourselves, but rather give place to wrath: for it is written, Vengeance is mine; I will repay, saith the Lord.)

43. **And the Lord said ...**, page 127, <u>Bible</u>, Luke 23:34, (Then said Jesus, "Father, forgive them, for they know not what they do.")

44. **And the Lord said ...**, page 127, <u>Bible</u>, Matthew 5:39, ("But I say unto you, That ye resist not evil: but whosoever shall smite thee on thy right cheek, turn to him the other also.")

45. **New World Twist**, page 129, <u>Bible</u>, Jonah 3:4-10, (... So the people of Nineveh believed God, and proclaimed a fast, and put on sackcloth, from the greatest of them even to the least of them. ... And God saw their works, that they turned from their evil way; and God repented of the evil, that He had said that He would do unto them; and He did it not.)

46. **Henry Wadsworth Longfellow**, Page 138, (American Poet; 27 February 1807 to 24 March 1882), excerpt from *The Ladder of St. Augustine*, (1858).

47. **Bob Nesta Marley**, Page 138, (Jamaican singer, song writer and musician; 6 February 1945 to 11 May 1981), excerpt of song lyric One Love/People Get Ready

For a copy of **The Contemplation of Harold**
please send your donation to:

Sterling Enterprises
6340 Lake Worth Blvd. # 243
Fort Worth, TX 76135

Or visit our website at:
WWW.CONTEMPLATIONOFHAROLD.COM

Printed in the USA
CPSIA information can be obtained
at www.ICGtesting.com
CBHW081619140124
3287CB00029B/9